YOGYAK
Travel Guide
2025-2026

What to See, Eat, Do &
Experience—Smart Tips, Hidden
Gems, Local Eats &
Budget-Friendly Adventures

Rosie G. Bacon

Table Of Content

5

YOGYAKARTA

Yogyakarta

Yogyakarta City, Special Region of
Yogyakarta, Indonesia

View larger map

Directions

Vredeburg Fort Museum

Taman
Yogyal

Taman Pintar Yogyakar

Ahmad Dahlan

Yogyakarta

Jl. Panembahan Senopa

Museum
Sonobudoyo Unit I

Bank Indonesia

Kantor Pelaya
Pratama Yogy

HOW TO USE QR CODE

1. Install a QR Code Scanner App.
2. Open the QR Code Scanner app.
3. Point your smartphone camera at the QR code you want to scan.
4. After successfully scanning the QR code, the app will often reveal the information within it.
5. Follow the prompt, and you're on your way.

7

INTRODUCTION

Welcome To Yogyakarta

Yogyakarta is a city in Southeast Asia that seamlessly combines the soul of ancient kingdoms, the fire of active volcanoes, the rhythm of street life, and the quiet wisdom of traditional communities. Perhaps you have never heard of it. Perhaps you scrolled past it while dreaming of Bali or Bangkok.

But let me tell you something, once you've visited Yogyakarta, you'll wonder why you didn't discover it sooner. This is more than just a city; it is Java's beating heart. It's where batik still tells stories, every shadow puppet has a soul, and the sunrise over Borobudur feels like a one-of-a-kind experience.

Yogyakarta welcomes everyone, whether you're a solo traveler seeking quiet adventures, a couple looking for romance in ancient ruins, a family eager to learn about culture through play, or a backpacker seeking meaning and magic. Yogyakarta reminds you to slow down in a world that is becoming increasingly fast-paced.

To drink your kopi joss from a roadside stall. To watch artisans work magic with their hands. To become lost—and then found—in alleyways adorned with murals, gamelan echoes, and genuine smiles.

A Brief History of Yogyakarta

Yogyakarta's story is told not only in museums and textbooks, but also in the streets, the sounds of the gamelan, and the quiet strength of the people who live there. To understand this city today, take a brief walk through its history.

Yogyakarta's roots extend deep into Java's ancient kingdoms. It was once part of the powerful Mataram Kingdom (8th-10th century), which created masterpieces such as Borobudur and Prambanan, which continue to awe visitors today. These were not just religious structures; they represented a thriving civilization fueled by art, trade, and spirituality.

Fast forward to the 18th century, when Yogyakarta as we know it was officially founded. Following a civil war in the Mataram Sultanate, the Kingdom was divided in 1755 by the Giyanti Agreement, establishing the Yogyakarta Sultanate. The royal palace, the Kraton, was established by the first Sultan, Hamengkubuwono

I, and it continues to serve as a cultural and spiritual hub. Even today, the royal family is actively involved in preserving local traditions, arts, and values.

Yogyakarta played a key role in Indonesia's independence struggle. It served as the nation's temporary capital from 1946 to 1949, after the Dutch occupied Jakarta. This move cemented its reputation as a hotbed of resistance, intellectualism, and nationalism. Yogyakarta was granted special region status in recognition of its loyalty and contribution to the country, making it the only part of Indonesia that is still officially ruled by a Sultan.

Yogyakarta is truly unique in that, while the world around it modernizes, it maintains its traditional roots. Here, ancient rituals coexist with street art. Traditional batik workshops sit alongside modern cafés. Ancient temples continue to attract those seeking both beauty and meaning.

So, when you visit Yogyakarta, you are not simply walking through a city; you are entering a living legacy. One that tells stories about empires, resistance, resilience, and creativity. And whether you're climbing temple steps at dawn or chatting with locals over kopi joss at night, that legacy will follow you — gently but profoundly.

Why Visit Yogyakarta in 2025

Borobudur Temple has reopened with new sustainable access, resulting in fewer crowds and richer experiences.

Travel infrastructure is better than ever, from modernized airport connections to improved local transportation.

More exciting cultural experiences, such as traditional dance classes and behind-the-scenes looks at Ramayana performances.

Rising art scenes and food markets are giving this ancient city a new vitality.

And, let's be honest: if you're looking for a place that feels underappreciated but a lifetime memory, this is it.

Who This Guide Is For

(Solo Travelers, Couples, Families, Backpackers)

This is not merely a guidebook. It's a useful companion for:

Solo Travelers: You'll discover safe places to explore, where to meet other travelers, and the best quiet places to unwind.

Couples: From romantic sunset views in Prambanan to secluded hillside cafés, we've got your love story covered.

Families: We highlight kid-friendly attractions, low-key dining options, and advice for traveling with small children.

Backpackers: This guide speaks your language when it comes to low-cost accommodations, local cuisine, and affordable experiences.

What Makes This Guide Unique

We created this book to give you

- Fresh, up-to-date information for 2025, including what is new, what has changed, and what is worthwhile.
- Local tips that you won't find on mainstream travel websites.

- Practical advice that addresses common travel questions (such as how to find a dependable driver or where to get Wi-Fi without purchasing a SIM card).
- Whether you're a foodie, history buff, thrill-seeker, or simply want to relax, we've got you covered.
- Most importantly, this guide was written to feel human, like a friend walking you through the city, not a robot spewing information at you.

How to Use This Book

Think of this book as a travel toolbox. Use it however you want. If you're short on time, skip straight to the Top Attractions.

If you want to dig deeper, go to the Hidden Gems section.

Use our custom itineraries to plan your days based on how long you'll be staying.

Need advice on safety, finances, or emergencies? Skip straight to the Practical Information section.

Each chapter is organized so that you can read it sequentially or as needed. We've also included QR codes and app suggestions to help you explore more efficiently and save time on the ground.

WHAT'S NEW IN YOGYAKARTA IN 2025

New Attractions & Developments

- Yogyakarta's classic charm will be enhanced by new experiences in 2025.
- A new eco-cultural park in Sleman celebrates Javanese village life through workshops, rice-field walks, and cultural performances — ideal for families and solo travelers seeking authenticity.
- In addition, the popular HeHa Sky View has expanded with new dining areas and photo opportunities for sunset enthusiasts and Instagram users.

Upgraded Infrastructure & Tourist Facilities

Yogyakarta International Airport (YIA) has improved transportation connections, including shuttle buses and improved train access.

Malioboro Street has been redesigned with wider sidewalks, clearer signage, and cleaner spaces, making it easier and safer to walk. M

Events, Festivals & Cultural Updates

The Yogyakarta Gamelan Festival and Wayang Week will return in 2025, with more international guests and performances in outdoor venues.

There's also a new monthly Night Market Festival, which includes food trucks, local crafts, and music — a great way to experience local life after sunset.

Trending Spots Among Locals & Expats

Locals and digital nomads are flocking to new cafes in the Prawirotaman neighborhood, a quiet yet trendy part of the city.

Boutique hostels and coworking cafés provide a relaxing atmosphere, excellent coffee, and fast Wi-Fi. Watu Goyang Viewpoint is gaining popularity among nature lovers as a peaceful alternative to the crowded Bukit Bintang.

PLANNING YOUR TRIP

Best Time to Visit

Yogyakarta has a tropical climate, which means it is warm and humid all year round. But timing your visit correctly can make a big difference.

The dry season (May to September) is generally the best time to visit, as it allows for sightseeing, hiking around Mount Merapi, and exploring temples such as Borobudur and Prambanan without getting soaked.

Festival season runs from June to August for culture lovers. Expect colorful parades, traditional performances, and vibrant local celebrations such as the Sekaten Festival, which revives royal traditions in the heart of the city.

If you don't mind a few showers and want to avoid the tourist crowds, the wet season (October to April) can provide lower prices and lush, green landscapes — just bring light rain gear.

Visa Requirements & Entry Tips

Indonesia welcomes tourists, and many nationalities can enter relatively easily. Citizens of over 90 countries will be able to enter without a visa for up to 30 days beginning in 2025. If you intend to stay longer or for special purposes (such as volunteering or business), you must apply for the appropriate visa in advance.

Make sure your passport is valid for at least six months after your entry date. Before you fly, always double-check visa requirements with an official Indonesian embassy or immigration website, as policies can change. Keep a printed or digital copy of your return ticket; immigration officers may request proof of departure.

How to Get to Yogyakarta

Yogyakarta is now more accessible than ever before, thanks to improved transportation and modern infrastructure. Whether you're flying in from abroad or driving across Java, there's an option to fit your schedule, comfort level, and budget.

By Air: Yogyakarta International Airport (YIA)

Yogyakarta International Airport (YIA), located about 45 kilometers (28 miles) west of the city center, is the primary entry point for most visitors. The airport is modern and well-equipped, accommodating both domestic and international flights.

Domestic Flights: Yogyakarta has frequent daily flights to Jakarta, Bali (Denpasar), Surabaya, and Medan. Airlines such as Garuda Indonesia, Lion Air, Citilink, and AirAsia provide competitive pricing.

Jakarta to Yogyakarta: $30-$70 USD, one-hour flight.

Bali to Yogyakarta: $45-$90 USD for a 1.5-hour flight.

International Flights: Direct international flights are readily available from Kuala Lumpur, Singapore, and Penang, primarily through AirAsia and Scoot. Expect to pay between $50 and $120 USD, depending on the season and how early you book.

Getting to the City

A car or shuttle ride from the airport to the city center takes about 1-1.5 hours. Options include:

DAMRI airport buses: (around $3 USD)

Taxis or Grab (ride-hailing): $10 to $20 USD, depending on traffic.

Airport Rail Link: A train connects YIA to Yogyakarta city via Wojo or Wates Station, followed by a transfer by local transport (total approximately $2-$4 USD).

By Train (Scenic, Affordable, and Comfortable)

If you're traveling from another part of the island of Java, train travel is an excellent option. The journey provides stunning views of rice fields, volcanoes, and villages.

From Jakarta (Gambir Station): 6-8 hours; prices range from $7 to $25 USD depending on the class.

Ekonomi (Economics): Basic but decent (from $7)

Bisnis (Business): More comfortable seating (starting from $15).

Eksekutif (Executive): Air-conditioned, reclining seats (from $20 to $25).

From Surabaya: 4-5 hours, from $6 to $20 USD. Trains arrive at Tugu Station, located in the heart of the city near Malioboro Street — an ideal location for first-time visitors. Bookings can be made via the KAI Access App, Tiket.com, or at the station. It is best to make reservations in advance, especially during holidays or weekends.

By Bus (Cheapest Option for Budget Travelers)

Buses are the most cost-effective way to get to Yogyakarta, but the journeys can be long and uncomfortable depending on traffic and road conditions.

From Jakarta: 10-12 hours; fares range from $10 to $20 USD.

From Surabaya or Malang: approximately 6-8 hours, from $8 to $15 USD.

Popular bus companies include Sumber Alam, Rosalia Indah, PO Haryanto, and Handoyo.

Many buses feature air conditioning, reclining seats, and rest stops. Some even offer snacks and blankets on overnight routes.

Buses usually arrive at Giwangan Bus Terminal, which is approximately 20 minutes from the city center. You can get to your hotel by taking a local taxi, an ojek (a motorcycle taxi), or Grab.

Budget Planning

One of Yogyakarta's greatest assets is affordability. Regardless of your travel style — shoestring budget or all-out luxury — the city provides exceptional value without compromising on experience. Here's how much you can expect to spend per day based on your travel preferences, along with practical information about where that money goes.

Backpackers and Budget Travelers ($20–$35/day)

Travelling on a tight budget? Yogyakarta is incredibly welcoming to backpackers.

Accommodation: Dorm beds in clean hostels and guesthouses start at $5 to $10 per night. Some even offer breakfast.

Food: Eat like a local with delicious street food (think satay, nasi gudeg, and mie ayam) for only $1-$2 per meal.

Transportation: Public buses or ride-sharing apps like Grab are inexpensive — most local rides cost less than $1 to $2.

Activities: include free attractions, walking tours, local markets, and temple sightseeing on your own to keep costs low.

You can have a rich cultural experience for a low cost, especially if you stick to local services and attractions.

Mid-Range Travelers ($40–$80/day)

If you want to be comfortable without going overboard, this collection provides a well-balanced experience.

Accommodation: Private rooms in guesthouses, boutique hostels, and 2-3 star hotels cost between $20 and $40 per night.

Food: A mix of local restaurants and cafés, with meals ranging from $3 to $10 depending on the location.

Transportation: More flexibility — consider renting a scooter ($5-$7 per day) or hiring a private driver for shorter trips.

Activities: include paid admission to temples (such as Borobudur and Prambanan), cultural performances, and guided group tours.

This budget allows you to explore deeper, dine better, and experience more of what Yogyakarta has to offer without breaking the bank.

Families or couples ($90-150 per day)

Planning a trip for two or with children? This range offers privacy and convenience.

Accommodation: Family suites or stylish hotels with pools and breakfast start around $50 to $80 per night.

Food: A comfortable meal at a clean, air-conditioned restaurant or hotel buffet costs $5-$15 per person.

Transport: Hire a full-day private driver for $30–$50/day, which is great for comfort and convenience with kids.

Add-on activities: include batik-making workshops, Ramayana ballet performances, and day trips to waterfalls or caves.

This style strikes a balance between comfort and cultural involvement, making it ideal for relaxing yet enriching travel.

Luxury Travelers ($200+/day)

Want a luxurious, selected experience? Yogyakarta delivers beautifully.

Accommodation: Boutique resorts, heritage hotels, and private villas start at $120 or more per night, and often include spa services, fine dining, and views.

Dining: Gourmet meals at fine restaurants, fusion dishes, or private dining experiences cost $20-$50 per person.

Transport options: include chauffeured vehicles, first-class train tickets, and even domestic flights for quick getaways.

Experiences: include private temple tours with sunrise access, customized art or cooking classes, and wellness retreats.

Yogyakarta's luxury scene is still in its early stages, but you can expect world-class service at a fraction of the cost of Bali or Singapore.

Final Tip

Plan for small extras like entrance fees (Borobudur: ~$25, Prambanan: ~$18), tipping (optional but appreciated), and souvenirs like batik or silver jewelry.

Your money goes a long way here, and meaningful experiences do not always come at a high cost.

What to Pack

Weather is hot, humid, and unpredictable. Whether you're visiting temples or hiking near volcanoes, what you bring can make or break your experience. Here's exactly what you need (and why):

Lightweight, breathable clothing: options include cotton, linen, and quick-dry fabrics. You will sweat a lot.

Dress modestly: When visiting temples or local communities, cover your shoulders and knees. A sarong or scarf is useful.

Comfortable shoes: You'll be walking around ruins, markets, and hills, so wear comfortable shoes. Closed-toed shoes or supportive sandals are best.

Sun protection: A good hat, sunglasses, and SPF 30+ sunscreen are essential — the sun is harsh here.

Rain gear: A foldable rain jacket or poncho is essential during the rainy season (October to April). Sudden downpours are common.

Reusable water bottle: Staying hydrated is essential, especially in the heat. Refill stations are easily accessible in cafes and hotels.

Insect repellent: Mosquitoes are prevalent, particularly in rural areas and during the rainy season. DEET-based repellents work the best.

Motion sickness tablets: Motion sickness tablets are useful if you're taking winding bus routes or going up into the hills (such as Mount Merapi).

Power adapter: Indonesia's plug types are C and F, with a standard voltage of 230V. Bring a universal adapter if necessary.

Optional, but helpful

Travel umbrella that serves as both a sun and rain shield.

Quick-dry towel is ideal for day trips to beaches or waterfalls.

A small backpack or day bag is ideal for exploring without having to carry your luggage.

Finally, leave the heavy clothing and bulky gear at home. In Yogyakarta, simplicity and practicality always prevail.

Travel Insurance & Why It's Important

Let's be honest, no one expects things to go wrong on vacation. But when they do, you'll be glad you purchased travel insurance. Yogyakarta may appear to be a peaceful, magical escape, but that does not mean it is without surprises. Whether your bag disappears on a train, a volcano hike results in a twisted ankle, or your flight is canceled at the last minute, insurance is your safety net. Medical care in Yogyakarta is adequate for minor ailments. Clinics are available in tourist areas, and hospitals such as RS Bethesda and Sardjito Hospital have a positive reputation. However, for more serious cases, you may be referred to Jakarta or even Singapore, and international treatment costs can quickly add up. A medevac alone can cost more than $20,000 USD if uninsured.

Here's what to look for in an effective policy

- Medical insurance (a minimum of $100,000 is ideal)
- Emergency evacuation and repatriation.
- Trip cancellations or interruptions
- Lost, stolen, or delayed baggage.
- Coverage for adventure activities such as volcano trekking, scooter riding, and surfing (many policies do not include this by default).
- COVID-19 coverage, including quarantine costs, if still applicable in 2025.

Pro tip: always read the fine print. Some insurers require you to wear a helmet while riding a motorcycle or use licensed tour operators for activities; otherwise, your claims may be denied. World Nomads, SafetyWing, and Allianz Global Assistance are three recommended providers that travelers frequently trust — but compare based on your needs and travel style.

Travel insurance is something you hope you never need, but if you do, it can save you both money and your trip.

GETTING AROUND YOGYAKARTA

Transportation Options

(Scooter, Taxi, Bus, GoJek)

Getting around Yogyakarta is easy, flexible, and budget-friendly. Whether you're traveling alone or with family, there are many ways to move from temples, neighborhoods, and food streets without breaking the bank.

Scooter Rental

If you're comfortable on two wheels, renting a scooter is the quickest and most flexible way to get around the city and its surroundings.

Cost: approximately IDR 75,000-110,000 per day ($5-$7 USD).

Where to rent: Many guesthouses and hostels rent bikes, and you can book ahead of time through apps like Traveloka and Klook, as well as local agencies like Jogja Rent Bike.

Requirements

- International Driver's Permit (IDP) and motorcycle license
- Valid passport

Tips: Always wear a helmet (you will receive one with the rental).

Drive defensively; local traffic can be unpredictable.

Fuel up yourself; petrol costs around IDR 10,000/liter (~$0.70) at roadside stalls

Taxis

Metered taxis are reliable, but they are not as frequently flagged down on the street. Blue Bird Taxi is the most trustworthy brand.

Cost: Minimum fare is IDR 8,000-10,000 ($0.50-$0.70).

The average 15-minute ride costs IDR 30,000-50,000 ($2-$3.50).

How To Book

- Download the MyBlueBird application.
- Ask your hotel receptionist to call one for you.

Avoid: unmarked taxis and those that refuse to use a meter.

Trans-Jogja Bus System

TransJogja is clean, air-conditioned, and runs efficiently throughout the city, making it ideal for budget-conscious travelers.

Cost: IDR 3,500 ($0.25 USD) per ride, regardless of distance.

How to Ride

- Purchase an e-ticket card (called Kartu Tiket Elektronik) for approximately IDR 20,000 ($1.30) at major bus stops.
- Top-up credit as needed.

Coverage

- Malioboro Street
- Prambanan Temple

- Adisutjipto and Yogyakarta International Airports

Buses run every 10-15 minutes, from approximately 5 AM to 9 PM.

Ideal for: Short city rides, budget travel, and those seeking a local experience.

GoJek & Grab (Ride-Hailing Apps)

Indonesia's Uber alternatives — GoJek and Grab — are absolute lifesavers. Both offer scooter taxis and private cars.

Cost (Go Ride/GrabBike)

Short ride (3-5 kilometres): IDR 10,000-15,000 ($0.70-$1 USD).

Cost of a GoCar or GrabCar

City trips cost IDR 20,000-40,000 ($1.50-$3 USD).

How To Book

- Get GoJek or Grab from the App Store or Google Play.
- Set your pick-up and drop-off points.
- Select your vehicle type (bike or car).
- Pay with cash or link your card/e-wallet.

Additional perks

Order food, groceries, or even massages using the apps.

Drivers are typically friendly and used to tourists

Practical informations

Apps to download before arrival include: GoJek, Grab, MyBlueBird, Google Maps, and Traveloka.

Cash or e-money: Keep small amounts of rupiah on hand to pay drivers or load your bus card.

Safety first: Avoid late-night travel in remote areas, and always double-check the license plate before getting into a car or bike.

Navigating the City Like a Local

Want to blend in with the locals rather than stand out like a lost tourist with a giant map? Yogyakarta makes it surprisingly simple. It's a city of rhythms, from scooter honks to friendly greetings from street vendors, and learning how to move with them will make your experience more enjoyable and memorable.

1. Learn a few Bahasa words

A little effort can go a long way. While many younger Indonesians speak basic English, especially in tourist areas:

- Terima kasih = Thank you
- Permisi = Excuse me
- Berapa harganya? = How much is it?
- Saya tidak mengerti = I don't understand

2. Be prepared to walk (and sweat)

Yogyakarta's charm stems from its street life, including murals, markets, and food stalls. Walk whenever possible, particularly around Malioboro Street and the Kraton area. Just remember:

- It's hot and humid, so wear light clothing and bring a refillable water bottle.
- Sidewalks may be uneven or missing, so sturdy sandals or sneakers are your best bet.

3. Use Google Maps and Local Apps

Google Maps works well in Yogyakarta, but combines it with GoJek or Grab for real-time rides and food delivery. Many locals use these apps for more than just transportation; they also buy groceries and send packages.

4. Understand the local traffic culture

Don't expect orderly traffic; more like organized chaos. Motorcyclists rule the road, and pedestrians are occasionally ignored. Cross the street slowly but confidently; cars are more likely to slow down if you are visible and assertive. Always remember to look both ways.

5. Pay like a local

Most street vendors and small businesses accept cash only. ATMs are widely available, and digital payment apps such as GoPay and OVO are increasingly popular. If you're paying with cash, keep small bills on hand—breaking a 100,000 IDR note for a $1 drink won't always go smoothly.

6. Follow Local Etiquette

- Smile often. It's part of everyday conversation here.
- Remove your shoes before entering homes or certain shops.
- Dress modestly, especially in temples and traditional neighborhoods.
- Avoid raising your voice in public or during negotiations; calm politeness always wins.

7. Know where you are going at night

The city is generally safe, even at night. However, not all areas are well-lit or busy after 9 p.m. Stick to well-known destinations, use ride-hailing apps after dark, and notify your lodging if you'll be leaving late.

Accessibility for Disabled Travelers

Yogyakarta is a charming and culturally rich city, but accessibility for disabled travelers is still evolving. While the city is not completely barrier-free, improvements are being made on a regular basis, and with proper planning, you can enjoy it with ease and confidence.

Public Attractions and Accessibility

Borobudur Temple and Prambanan Temple: Are partially accessible. The upper levels of Borobudur are inaccessible due to steep ancient steps, but the ground-level museum, visitor center, and surrounding park are paved and mostly flat.

Wheelchair rental: Borobudur offers wheelchair rentals for around IDR 100,000/day (~$6.50 USD), which can be requested at the main entrance ticket counter.

Entry fee: For foreigners, the entry fee is IDR 375,000 (~$24 USD). Companions may be eligible for a discount.

How to get there

A private driver or taxi is the best option. It is approximately 45 minutes from central Yogyakarta.

Hiring a private van for a day costs approximately IDR 500,000-700,000 ($32-$45 USD).

For easier vehicle access, contact a reputable transportation provider such as Jaya Transport (WhatsApp: +62 812 2666 1116).

Taman Sari (Water Castle) and Kraton Palace: Are culturally fascinating, but the pathways are narrow and the surfaces uneven.

Hiring a local private guide (IDR 100,000-150,000 or ~$6-$10 for a half-day) can help you navigate safely.

How to get there

Both are in the city center (around 10-15 minutes by car from most hotels).

Use GoJek or Grab for short rides ranging from IDR 10,000-30,000 (~$0.65-$2 USD).

Tip: Inquire about side entrances or hidden ramps, as they may not always be visible.

Hotels & Accommodations

Accessible rooms are most common in mid-range and luxury hotels, particularly those built or renovated after 2015.

Hyatt Regency Yogyakarta

- Wheelchair-accessible rooms, ramps, elevators, and large grounds.

Price: IDR 900,000-1,200,000 per night (~$58-$80 USD).

The Phoenix Hotel Yogyakarta

- Historic colonial-style hotel with step-free access, elevators, and accessible bathrooms.

Price: IDR 750,000-1,000,000 per night (approximately $48-$65 USD).

Here's how to get there

From the Yogyakarta International Airport (YIA)

- Private airport transfers cost approximately IDR 300,000-400,000 (~$20-$26 USD) for a car or van.
- Hotel shuttles (provided by some hotels) can be pre-booked; always request assistance or a vehicle with extra space if necessary.

Transportation and Getting Around

Private drivers with vans

- Best option for travelers who require wheelchair access or assistance with boarding.
- Private van rental companies include Jaya Transport and Yogyakarta Private Tours.

Cost: IDR 500,000-700,000 per day (approximately $32-$45 USD).

GoJek and Grab apps

- City trips are both affordable and flexible.
- There are currently no wheelchair-adapted vehicles, only standard cars.

Local city rides cost between IDR 10,000-30,000 (~$0.65-$2 USD).

Tip: If you need assistance folding and storing a wheelchair, contact the driver via the app.

Navigation of Streets and Sidewalks

- Sidewalks may be narrow, uneven, or occasionally obstructed by motorcycles and vendors.
- Mornings (7-10 AM) and late afternoons (after 4 PM) are quieter and cooler, making them ideal for exploration.

Hiring a local assistant for around IDR 100,000-200,000/day (~$6.50-$13 USD) can provide much-needed mobility support in busy areas.

Medical Facilities and Emergency Support

RSUP Dr. Sardjito (Public Hospital)

- Wheelchair-accessible with 24-hour emergency services.

Location: Jalan Kesehatan No. 1, Sleman.

Phone number: +62 274 587333.

Here's how to get there

About 20 minutes from central Yogyakarta. The best option is to use a private car or taxi. Grab rides typically cost between IDR 30,000-50,000 (~$2-$3.50 USD).

Jogja International Hospital (JIH) (a private hospital)

- Modern facilities, English-speaking doctors, and easy access.

Location: Jl. Ring Road Utara No. 160, Condongcatur.

Phone number: +62 274 446 3535.

Here's how to get there

Approximately 25-30 minutes from most city hotels. Use Grab, GoJek, or a private driver.

Tip: Bring all important medications in your carry-on and a translated doctor's note for customs if needed.

Top Travel Tips for Disabled Visitors

- Bring a lightweight, foldable wheelchair if possible. Foldable travel ramps can also be used on small curbs.
- Essential apps include Google Maps (download offline maps), GoJek, Grab, and Google Translate.
- To avoid crowds and tropical heat, plan visits in the early mornings or after 4 p.m.

Final Thought

Yogyakarta isn't perfect in terms of accessibility, but what it lacks in infrastructure, it more than makes up for in kindness. Locals are incredibly helpful, and with some planning and flexibility, disabled visitors can truly experience the rich art, history, and soul of this magical city. Your adventure is waiting for you, and there's always someone to help you along the way.

Public Transport in Yogyakarta

Once you understand your options, getting around Yogyakarta can be relatively inexpensive and simple. The city provides a variety of modes of transportation, including public buses, private minibuses, and ride-hailing apps, each with its own set of characteristics. Here's everything you need to know to ride like a local (without stress!).

Trans-Jogja Bus System

TransJogja is Yogyakarta's official bus rapid transit system, which is safe, affordable, air-conditioned, and surprisingly efficient by Southeast Asia standards.

Cost: IDR 3,500 (~$0.23 USD) per ride, flat rate.

Operation Hours: Daily hours of operation are 6 a.m. to 9 p.m.

Payment: Pay with cash at the bus stop (halte) or purchase a prepaid card (around IDR 50,000 or ~$3.20 including initial balance) for convenient access.

Frequency: Buses arrive every 10-15 minutes during busy hours.

Routes

- Cover major locations such as Malioboro Street, Gadjah Mada University, Tugu Train Station, and Adisutjipto Airport.
- Some lines even connect to major shopping malls like Plaza Ambarrukmo and tourist attractions like Prambanan Temple (with transfers).

How to get there

- Bus stops (called halte) are easily identifiable as small, green shelters located on major roads.
- Popular halts include Malioboro 1, Terminal Giwangan, and Adisutjipto Airport Shelter.
- Google Maps works well for finding bus routes; simply enter your destination and select "Public Transport."

Tip: Always check the direction before boarding, as some lines loop in two directions.

City Minibuses (Angkot/Kopaja)

The colorful, minibus-like vehicles that roam the streets are known as angkot or kopaja—they are very local, cheap, and adventurous.

Cost ranges: From IDR 4,000-7,000 (~$0.25-$0.45 USD) based on distance.

Payment: Cash only — give it to the driver when you get off.

Operating hours: Are 5:30 a.m. to 7 p.m., sometimes later on busy routes.

How to ride

- Wave down an angkot from the roadside.
- Tell the driver where you want to go (or say "Kiri!" to signal a stop).
- They do not adhere to strict schedules and they leave when full.

Advantages: Extremely cheap and authentic.

Cons: Can be cramped, no air conditioning, and no predetermined routes/maps.

Ojek (motorcycle taxis) and app-based services

Ojek: Traditional motorcycle taxis are available on street corners.

GoJek and Grab: Safer and cheaper — book through the app, see the price upfront, and even pay cashless.

Cost Estimate

- Short rides (2-4 km) cost IDR 8,000-15,000 (approximately $0.50-1 USD).
- Airport rides to downtown (10-12 km) cost IDR 40,000-60,000 (~$2.50-$4 USD).

Tip: If you have luggage or need extra help, choose GrabCar or GoCar instead of bikes.

Taxi Services

- Blue Bird Taxi is the most dependable traditional taxi company.
- Metered fare starts at IDR 7,500 (~$0.50 USD) + IDR 4,000/km (~$0.25 USD/km).

You can hail a taxi on the street or book one through the MyBluebird app.

Airport to City Centre: Prices range from IDR 80,000-120,000 (~$5-$8 USD) based on hotel location.

Tips for Using Public Transportation in Yogyakarta

Download Essential Apps

- Google Maps works surprisingly well with TransJogja routes.
- GoJek and Grab offer instant motorcycle and car rides.
- MyBluebird: For taxi reservations.

Carry small amounts of cash

- Drivers frequently cannot provide change for large bills (anything over IDR 50,000).

Expect some heat

- Except for TransJogja and taxis, most local transportation lacks air conditioning. If you're taking an angkot minibus, bring a small towel or a fan.

Plan for extra time

- Public buses and minibuses can become stuck in traffic, particularly between 3-6 p.m. during the evening rush.

Practical information

Yogyakarta's public transportation is more than just a mode of transportation; it's an exciting part of the experience! Whether you board a TransJogja bus or ride a colorful angkot, you'll be experiencing the city's heartbeat at ground level. Simply bring a smile, some patience, and a few small bills, and you'll fit right in.

Hiring a Private Driver or Guide

Sometimes the best way to experience Yogyakarta's magic is with a little assistance from someone who knows the roads—and shortcuts—better than any app. Hiring a private driver or local guide can save you time, reduce travel stress, and allow you to explore parts of the city and countryside that you would otherwise miss. Here's what you should know:

Why hire a private driver or guide?

Convenience: No need to worry about bus schedules, confusing maps, or getting lost in an alley without Wi-Fi.

Comfort: Enjoy the comfort of an air-conditioned car while someone handles the unpredictable traffic in Yogyakarta.

Flexibility: Want to see Borobudur at sunrise, explore a hidden batik village, and watch the sunset at Parangtritis Beach? Simple — set your own schedule.

Local Insight: A knowledgeable guide can provide unique insights, such as stories, history, and local tips, that cannot be found in guidebooks.

Reliable drivers and guides can be found at hotels or guesthouses.

Where to Find Reliable Drivers and Guides

Hotel or Guesthouse

Most hotels recommend reliable drivers, who frequently offer packaged tours to Borobudur, Prambanan, and other city attractions.

Prices might be a bit higher but usually come with more reliability.

Travel Agency

Many agencies in tourist areas, such as Malioboro Street and Prawirotaman, provide private tours.

You can book on the same day or make arrangements ahead of time.

Online Platforms

Websites such as GetYourGuide, Klook, and Traveloka provide private car rentals or driver-guide services with reviews and fixed prices.

Some drivers advertise their services through Facebook groups or WhatsApp.

Word of mouth

Talk to other travelers or locals—some of the best drivers are booked weeks in advance due to strong personal recommendations.

Estimated Prices for Hiring a Driver or Guide

Half-day (4-5 hours): IDR 300,000-450,000 (\$20-$30 USD).

Full-day (8-10 hours): IDR 500,000-800,000 (\$33-$53 USD).

Sunrise tours, such as Borobudur Sunrise, may incur an additional cost of around IDR 600,000-1,000,000 (~$40-$66 USD), which includes early pickup.

What is included?

- Car Rental
- Fuel
- Driver's Fee
- Parking fees
- Bottled water (occasionally).

Not usually included

- Entrance fees for attractions
- Personal meals

Tip: Always confirm what's included before getting into the car.

Hiring a guide separately

If you prefer to drive yourself or take a taxi but still want a historical or cultural expert with you:

Certified guides can be hired at major tourist destinations such as Borobudur and Prambanan.

Rates range: From IDR 150,000-250,000 (~$10-$17 USD) per tour (1-2 hours).

Many guides speak good English, and some also offer tours in French, German, Japanese, and Korean.

Fun Option: Some private guides also provide photography tours, culinary adventures, and hidden village walks, which are ideal for those seeking something less touristy.

Important Tips Before Hiring

Check Reviews: When booking online, look for drivers or guides who have received many positive reviews and communicate effectively.

Discuss your plan first: Make it clear where you want to go and whether you want any "extra stops" (such as batik shops or silver factories). Some drivers receive commissions; if you're interested, say yes; otherwise, politely decline.

Set a price before starting: Avoid misunderstandings later. A good driver is always upfront.

Confirm air conditioning: Yogyakarta can be extremely hot and humid, particularly at midday. Confirm that you will receive a car that is properly air-conditioned.

Bring Cash: Most drivers prefer cash payment in Indonesian Rupiah.

When Hiring a Driver Makes Most Sense

- Hiring a driver makes sense for Borobudur and Prambanan day trips.
- Visiting these two sites in one day is more convenient with a private car.
- **Exploring Rural Villages and Beaches** Public transport doesn't reach places like Timang Beach, Imogiri Royal Tombs, or Kalibiru National Park easily.
- **Short Trips:** If you only have 1-2 days in Yogyakarta, hiring a driver can help you make the most of your sightseeing time.
- **Traveling with family or groups:** More convenient (and frequently cheaper) than booking multiple taxis or separate tours.

Practical information

Hiring a private driver or guide in Yogyakarta is more than just convenient; it's also an opportunity to experience Java's warm hospitality firsthand. Many travelers conclude their trip by saying their driver became a friend, sharing jokes, local tips, and stories that made their journey memorable.

Whether you're racing the sunrise at Borobudur, searching for hidden waterfalls, or simply trying to beat the heat, having a local by your side makes the journey all the more enjoyable.

Cycling & Walking Around

Exploring Yogyakarta by bike or on foot is one of the most enriching ways to experience the city's rhythm. Cycling and walking allow you to discover the heart of local life that you'd miss if you drove by. While not every street is ideal for pedestrians or cyclists, many routes are pleasant and scenic, particularly in the early morning or late afternoon.

Cycling in Yogyakarta

Cycling is popular among both tourists and locals—and for good reason. The flat terrain, short distances between attractions, and picturesque surroundings make it an excellent alternative to motorized transportation.

Where to Rent Bicycles

ViaVia Jogja Jl. Prawirotaman No.30

Open daily from 7 AM to 8 PM.

Standard bikes cost IDR 30,000/day ($2 USD), while mountain bikes cost IDR 50,000/day ($3.25 USD).

Jogja Bike Rental

Book online via WhatsApp at +62 822 2722 8020.

Offers delivery to your hotel.

City bikes cost IDR 25,000-40,000 per day.

Request multi-day discounts or guided cycling tours.

Best Cycle Routes

Taman Sari to Kotagede: A 5- to 6-kilometer ride through quiet kampung neighborhoods, historic buildings, and silver artisan shops.

Prawirotaman to Alun-Alun Kidul: A leisurely 20-minute ride, best in the early morning or after 4pm

Village Cycling in Kalibiru or Nanggulan (outside the city)

Hire a guide or join a cycling tour for around IDR 150,000-300,000 (~$10-$20), including rental, guide, and snacks.

Note: Always wear a helmet (usually provided), avoid riding after dark, and be cautious of potholes and scooters that do not always follow traffic rules.

Walking in Yogyakarta

Walking is not only free, but also exciting. Strolls reveal murals, street warungs (food stalls), and locals going about their business. While sidewalks are not always reliable, some areas are ideal for pedestrians.

Top walkable areas

Malioboro Street: The most well-known pedestrian zone in Yogyakarta. Recent renovations included wider sidewalks, public seating, and ramps. Expect crowds, vendors, and a lively energy. Best visited in the evening.

Getting there: Easily accessible via TransJogja (route 1A or 2B), GoJek, or taxi.

Distance: Approximately 1 km from Tugu Station to Beringharjo Market.

Prawirotaman and Tirtodipuran Boutique hotels, galleries, and quiet cafés make this a relaxing, creative neighborhood to explore on foot. A beautiful spot for morning walks.

Alun-alun Selatan (Southern Square): Food carts, music, and blinking pedal cars make for a particularly lively nightlife. The sidewalks here are manageable, but watch out for crowds.

Tip: Use the Maps.me app for offline walking maps or Google Maps' pedestrian mode for safe navigation.

Safety and Local Tips

- The best times to explore are before 10 a.m. or after 4 p.m. to avoid the midday heat.
- Wear comfortable shoes as many sidewalks are uneven and abruptly end.
- Bring sunscreen, a refillable water bottle, and an umbrella (for sun and rain).
- Be cautious crossing streets. Use pedestrian crossings when possible, and make eye contact with drivers before exiting.

Combining walking and biking with public transportation.

You can bring a folding bike on TransJogja buses, particularly during off-peak hours.

Walk to larger landmarks and then take a GoJek/Grab to your next destination if the heat becomes too much.

Guided cycling and walking tours typically include pick-up/drop-off and range in cost from IDR 150,000-400,000 (~$10-$26 USD), depending on duration and group size.

Final Thought

Cycling and walking around Yogyakarta not only transports you from point A to point B, but also allows you to connect deeply with the city's rhythm, people, and surprises. Whether you're gliding past rice fields on a bike or discovering a hidden batik shop on foot, these slow travel methods reward the intrepid traveler.

Local Laws, & Safety Tips For Getting Around YogyakartaYogyakarta is warm, welcoming, and generally safe, but there are still a few important things to keep in mind while exploring. Here's your no-fuss guide to staying respectful, safe, and stress-free as you get around this beautiful city.

Local Laws to Know (So You Don't Get Into Trouble)

What's the Rule?

Carry ID: Keep a copy of your passport on you (or a clear photo on your phone). Just in case local authorities ask.

Dress modestly at temples & sacred sites: Shoulders and knees covered = respectful.

Drugs are 100% illegal: Seriously, even tiny amounts can mean jail time. Don't risk it.

Drink alcohol discreetly: Bars, restaurants, or your hotel are okay. Avoid public drinking, especially near religious places.

Don't smoke everywhere: Smoking's fine outdoors, but not in malls, temples, or on buses. Look for signs.

Driving? You need an IDP: That's an International Driving Permit. Police do random stops, especially with tourists on scooters.

Smart Safety Tips for Travelers

Stick to trusted transport: Use Grab or GoJek (the apps), or ask your hotel to call a reliable driver. Avoid random taxis, they might overcharge.

Look both ways — always: Even on one-way streets, scooters can surprise you. Traffic doesn't always follow the rules.

Keep an eye on your stuff: Pickpocketing isn't common, but crowded spots like Malioboro Street attract opportunists. Don't flash valuables.

Sidewalks can be unpredictable: Some are broken, blocked, or just vanish. Wear comfy shoes, and take your time — especially at night.

Don't buy tickets from strangers: That "too good to be true" tour? It probably is. Get your tickets online or at official counters only.

Crossing the road? Be bold (but safe): Pedestrian crossings are suggestions here — make eye contact with drivers before stepping out. Or cross with locals.

If You Need Help Who to Call

You're lost or need police help

- *Tourist Police (Malioboro):* +62 274 563974

Emergency, urgent situation

- *General Police (Polresta):* 110 or +62 274 543362

Medical emergency, Jogja International

- *Hospital:* +62 274 4463535

Lost passport

Your Embassy or Consulate: (Most are in Jakarta, keep digital copies!)

Travel Tip: Ask your hotel to write its name and address in Bahasa Indonesia for you — this makes it easy to show drivers or locals if you get turned around.

Quick Tips for Getting Around Smoothly

Keep small bills (IDR 2,000–20,000) for local transport, tips, and quick snacks.

Download Google Translate and offline maps before you go out.

If you're walking or cycling, early mornings (7–10 AM) or late afternoons (after 4 PM) are the most pleasant times — fewer crowds, less heat.

Don't hesitate to ask locals for help — Javanese people are kind and happy to assist (often with a smile).

Practical information

Getting around Yogyakarta is mostly smooth and safe — just stay aware, respect the culture, and use a bit of common sense. You'll quickly find that people here are more than willing to help you along the way.

Keep your curiosity high, your bag zipped, and your heart open — and Yogyakarta will treat you well.

WHERE TO STAY

Best Neighborhoods for Tourists

Choosing where to stay in Yogyakarta can really shape your experience — whether you want to be in the middle of the action, surrounded by art and cafés, or waking up to mountain air and the smell of trees. Here's a guide to the best areas to base yourself in, depending on what kind of trip you're after.

Malioboro

Why you'll love it: This is Yogyakarta's most iconic area — always buzzing with life. It's great for those who want to be right in the heart of it all. Markets, museums, historical sites, batik stalls, food carts — you'll find them all within walking distance.

The vibe: Busy, energetic, full of color, very tourist-friendly.

What's around

- Kraton Palace
- Taman Sari Water Castle
- Malioboro Mall
- Night markets & street food galore

Good for: First-timers, families, culture lovers, anyone who doesn't mind the crowds.

Price range

Budget: \~IDR 150,000–300,000/night (\$10–\$20)

Mid-range: \~IDR 400,000–800,000/night (\$25–\$50)

Getting there

- *From the airport:* Grab or GoCar (IDR 60,000–80,000), or TransJogja bus Line 1A

Prawirotaman

Why you'll love it: Think of it as the "hipster district" of Jogja. Stylish cafés, art shops, hostels with pools, murals on the walls — it's chill and full of character.

The vibe: Artsy, modern, laid-back — with a touch of Bali-like energy.

What's around

- Cool cafés, vegan-friendly restaurants
- Boutique shops
- Yoga studios and galleries
- Just 10–15 minutes from the palace by motorbike

Good for: Solo travelers, couples, digital nomads, creative types.

Price range

Budget stays from IDR 100,000/night

Mid-range hotels up to IDR 600,000/night (\$7–\$40)

How to get there

- 10–15 minutes from Malioboro by Grab or GoJek (IDR 15,000–25,000)

Kaliurang

Why you'll love it: Up in the hills near Mt. Merapi, this area offers cooler air and a much-needed break from city noise. It's also the launchpad for volcano tours and nature walks.

The vibe: Calm, scenic, sometimes misty in the morning — perfect for early risers and mountain souls.

What's around

- Mount Merapi Jeep tours
- Ullen Sentalu Museum (a local gem)
- Kaliurang Park and forest trails

Good for: Families, hikers, couples looking for a quiet escape.

Price range

Guesthouses from IDR 200,000

Private villas from IDR 500,000+

How to get there

- Around 1 hour from the city — best with a private driver or tour guide.

Gejayan & Sagan

Why you'll love it: These neighborhoods aren't flashy, but they're real. Full of student energy, local food, indie shops, and very affordable stays. If you want to feel like a local — this is it.

The vibe: Youthful, chill, budget-friendly.

What's around

- Gadjah Mada University
- Street food stalls (especially Angkringan)
- Coffee shops and night snacks

Good for: Budget travelers, students, long-stay visitors.

Price range

Hostels from IDR 60,000

Guesthouses from IDR 150,000–250,000/night

Getting there

- Grab or GoJek from anywhere in the city (\~IDR 15,000–20,000)

Kotagede

Why you'll love it: This is Yogyakarta's old town — peaceful, charming, and full of tradition. It's known for silverwork, ancient houses, and friendly locals. If you want to slow down, this is your place.

The vibe: Historical, elegant, sleepy in the best way.

What's around

- Traditional markets
- Batik houses and silver shops
- Ancient mosques and quiet alleys

Good for: Couples, culture lovers, travelers who prefer slow travel.

Price range

Homestays and heritage houses: IDR 200,000–400,000/night

- Best by Grab, GoJek, or motorbike (\~IDR 25,000 from city center)

Budget Stays & Backpacker Hostels

If you're the kind of traveler who'd rather spend on experiences than expensive beds, Yogyakarta has your back. The city is full of hostels and guesthouses that are not only super affordable but also full of charm and character. Whether you want to be near the buzz of Malioboro or in a laid-back artsy corner like Prawirotaman, there's a budget stay here that'll feel just right.

Where Budget Travelers Feel at Home

Sosrowijayan

Just off Malioboro Street, this is Yogyakarta's original backpacker zone. It's got everything: street food, cheap batik shops, hostels, and a real mix of travelers.

Prawirotaman

Think boho cafes, art murals, and a chill vibe. Great for slow mornings and longer stays.

Kraton & Mantrijeron

Closer to the palace and local life. A bit quieter, but still close to everything.

Top Budget-Friendly Hostels

The Packer Lodge Yogyakarta

Location: Sosrowijayan, near Malioboro

Price: From IDR 120,000 (\~\$8) for a comfy dorm bed

Why You'll Like It: Clean, modern, with great AC, hot showers, and a social vibe without being rowdy.

How to get there

- *Walkable from:* Tugu Train Station (about 10 mins)

YIA Airport: Take the DAMRI bus to Malioboro, then walk a few minutes

Giwangan Bus Terminal: Catch TransJogja Line 3B, stop at Malioboro 1, then walk

EDU Hostel

Location: Ngampilan (Near Kraton and the palace)

Price: From IDR 90,000 (\~\$6)

Why You'll Like It: It's big, colorful, and has a rooftop pool (!) and amazing views of the city skyline.

How to get there

- *From Tugu Station:* Grab or GoCar (IDR 20,000 or less)
- *From YIA Airport:* DAMRI bus to city center, then Grab
- *From Giwangan Terminal:* TransJogja Line 2A →Get off at Ngabean, walk 10 mins

Good Karma Yogyakarta

Location: Prawirotaman 1

Price: From IDR 100,000 for a dorm / IDR 180,000 for a private

Why You'll Like It

Laid-back, artistic, and friendly. Great common areas and vegetarian-friendly breakfasts.

<u>How to get there</u>

- *From Tugu Station:* GoCar or Grab (\~IDR 30,000)
- *From Giwangan:* TransJogja Line 3A, stop near Prawirotaman
- *From YIA Airport:* DAMRI bus to Prawirotaman or Grab (expect around IDR 90,000–100,000)

OstiC House

Location: Suryodiningratan (Mantrijeron)

Price: From IDR 130,000

Why Stay here: It's small, peaceful, and the kind of place where staff remember your name. Perfect for solo travelers.

How to get there

- *Grab from Tugu Station:* (\~IDR 25,000–30,000)
- TransJogja Line 3A to Suryodiningratan stop

The Capsule Malioboro

Location: Right by Malioboro Street, Sosrowijayan

Price: From IDR 110,000 for a spacey capsule

Best For: Privacy in a pod, modern vibes, and super close to all the action

How to get there

- Just 10 minutes' walk from Tugu Station
- *From YIA Airport:* DAMRI to Malioboro
- TransJogja Line 1A to Malioboro

Practical information

You don't have to splurge to stay somewhere cool in Yogyakarta. These hostels are clean, welcoming, and in all the right locations — so whether you're chasing temples or chilling in a hammock, you're covered.

Mid-Range Hotels for Comfort Seekers

Not into hostels but don't want to splurge on luxury either? You're in luck. Yogyakarta has a sweet spot of mid-range hotels that offer both comfort and style—without emptying your wallet. Whether you're a couple looking for a cozy getaway, a family who needs some space, or a solo traveler who just wants a proper bed and a hot shower, there's something here for you.

Best Areas to Look

Prawirotaman & Tirtodipuran

These are the artsy, laid-back neighborhoods filled with cool cafés, batik shops, and yoga studios. A favorite among creative travelers.

Malioboro Area

Perfect if you want to be near the hustle and bustle, street vendors, and shopping streets.

Kota Gede

A bit quieter, with a historical soul and beautiful silver workshops around every corner.

Top Mid-Range Places to Stay

Adhisthana Hotel

Location: Prawirotaman

Cost: From IDR 400,000 (\~\$25) a night.

Why You'll Like It: It's stylish, has Instagram-worthy design, a lovely little pool, and a nice café that serves real coffee.

How to get there

- Grab or Gojek from Tugu Station (around 25–30 mins)
- From YIA Airport, you can take a DAMRI bus to Taman Siswa, then hop in a Grab (or walk if you're up for it)

Greenhost Boutique Hotel

Location: Prawirotaman

Cost: From IDR 500,000 (\~\$33)

What Makes It Cool: Think eco-friendly vibes with greenery everywhere, a rooftop garden, and a creative space. It feels like a mini urban jungle.

How to get there

- Grab or TransJogja Line 3A to the Tirtodipuran area
- Around 30 minutes from Tugu Station

Gallery Prawirotaman Hotel

Location: Prawirotaman

Cost: From IDR 600,000 (\~\$40)

Why Stay Here: Comfy modern rooms, a relaxing pool, and it's within walking distance to great restaurants and coffee shops.

How to get there

- Grab or TransJogja Line 3A

Jogja Village Villa

Location: Mantrijeron (south of the palace)

Cost: From IDR 550,000 (\~\$36)

Feels Like: A peaceful garden oasis with traditional Javanese charm, perfect for those who want a break from city buzz.

How to get there

- Take TransJogja Line 3B to Mantrijeron
- Or Grab from Malioboro (\~20 mins)

What You Usually Get at This Price

- Air-conditioning (very welcome after a day in the sun!)
- Private bathrooms and clean, cozy rooms
- Free breakfast—usually nasi goreng, toast, fruit, and coffee
- Pool access in many cases
- Friendly staff and a travel desk to help plan your Borobudur or Merapi adventures
- Optional airport transfers (usually for a small extra fee)

Luxury Resorts & Romantic Retreats

Sometimes, you just want to press pause on real life. Whether you're on your honeymoon, celebrating something special, or simply craving a few nights of bliss, Yogyakarta has a handful of magical places that know how to treat you right. We're talking private villas, candlelit dinners with volcano views, and staff who remember how you like your coffee.

These aren't just hotels—they're unforgettable experiences. Here's where to find your slice of paradise.

Where to Stay for That Dreamy Luxury Escape

Borobudur Area

A quiet, green escape just outside the city, with stunning sunrise views and peaceful vibes.

Taman Sari & South Kraton

Stay near the royal palace in artsy, charming neighborhoods that feel like stepping into another time.

Kota Baru / Central City

More modern and convenient, close to shops and restaurants.

Kalasan & Prambanan

Stay near ancient temples in scenic, rural surroundings.

Top Luxury Stays in yogyakarta

Amanjiwo Resort

Location: Borobudur (Magelang)
Price: From IDR 10,000,000 (\~\$650) per night
Why It's Special: Set in the hills with views of Borobudur, it's a retreat where

everything—from your yoga mat to your sunset cocktails—is taken care of. Privacy and peace like nowhere else.

How to get there

- From Yogyakarta Int'l Airport (YIA): 1.5 hrs by private car, around IDR 400,000–600,000 (\$25–\$40)
- Many guests arrange hotel pickup—it's part of the pampering.

Plataran Borobudur Resort & Spa

Location: Near Borobudur Temple

Price: From IDR 4,000,000 (\~\$260) per night

Why It's Special: Elegant villas, spa treatments, and sunrise views over ancient ruins—this place blends Javanese heritage with luxury.

How to get there

- Around 1.5–2 hrs from central Yogyakarta by Grab or private car: IDR 300,000–500,000 (\$20–\$35)
- The hotel often offers shuttle service—just ask when you book.

Hyatt Regency Yogyakarta

Location: Sleman (Northwest Yogyakarta)

Rate: From IDR 1,500,000 (\~\$100) per night

Why It's Special: Set on a massive property with tropical gardens, a golf course, and a huge pool with a water slide—perfect for couples and families.

How to get there

- From Malioboro by TransJogja (Line 2A) IDR 3,500 (\$0.25), about 30 mins
- *By Grab:* IDR 30,000–50,000 (\$2–\$3.50)
- *From YIA:* about IDR 250,000 (\$16) by Grab or taxi

The Phoenix Hotel (MGallery Collection)

Location: Near Tugu Monument, central Yogyakarta

Rate: From IDR 1,200,000 (\~\$80) per night

Why It's Special: An elegant historic hotel with tiled floors, vintage décor, and a romantic old-world vibe. Think Downton Abbey with a Javanese twist.

How to get there

- 5-minute walk from Tugu Train Station

- *From YIA Airport by DAMRI shuttle*
  IDR 70,000 (\$4.50), about 1 hour
- *By Grab or taxi:* IDR 200,000–250,000
  (\$13–\$16)

Villa Rosseno

Location: Bantul (south of Yogyakarta)
Rate: From IDR 1,800,000 (\~\$120)
per night
Why It's Special: A hidden gem with
personal chefs, your own pool, and
lush greenery all around.
Perfect for couples who want something peaceful and
personal.

How to get there

- About 30–40 minutes from the city center by
  Grab. IDR 35,000–60,000 (\$2.50–\$4)
- The hosts can also arrange pickup if you prefer
  a smoother ride

What You Can Expect at These Luxury Spots

- Stylish, spacious rooms (many with private
  pools or jacuzzis)
- On-site restaurants with wine lists and locally
  sourced menus

- Spa services, wellness programs, and yoga classes
- Quiet surroundings—perfect for recharging
- Personalized attention, from flowers on the bed to tours curated just for you
- Most offer transport help or even airport pickup

Let them know if you're celebrating something—birthdays, anniversaries, honeymoons. Yogyakarta's luxury hotels love making your stay extra special (think rose petals, cakes, or even a surprise upgrade!).

Unique Stays

Eco-Lodges, Batik Homes & Heritage Houses

Sometimes, a place to sleep can become the reason you remember the trip forever. In Yogyakarta, you don't have to settle for just any hotel room. You can wake up to mist-covered rice fields, fall asleep under the roof of a 100-year-old joglo house, or sip your morning coffee while chatting with a local batik artist in their garden.

These aren't just places to stay—they're experiences wrapped in wood, warmth, and wonder.

Where to Find These Special Stays

Kasongan & Bantul

Full of artisan villages and quiet rice paddies

Kaliurang & Sleman

Found in the hills near Mount Merapi

Kotagede

Yogyakarta's old soul, where time slows down

Imogiri

Green, peaceful, and full of traditional life

Borobudur

Perfect for countryside calm and temple sunrises

Handpicked Stays That Feel Like Home (or Better!)

Joglo Plawang Boutique Villa

Location: Kaliurang (north of Yogyakarta)

Price: From IDR 1,100,000 (\~\$72) per night

Why You Will Love It: It's like staying in a dreamy, open-air museum. Traditional Javanese wood carvings, lush greenery all around, and the kind of quiet you didn't know you needed.

How to get there

- About 45–60 minutes by Grab from Malioboro, costs around IDR 60,000–80,000 (\$4–\$6)
- Public transport is tricky here—Grab or a rental is best.

Rumah Roso

Location: Prawirotaman (close to cafes and local life)

Price: From IDR 300,000 (\~\$20) per night

Why You'll We Love It: It's cozy, artsy, and feels like staying with a creative aunt who serves tea and teaches you batik. Great for solo travelers and couples.

How to get there

- Just 15–20 minutes from Tugu Station by Grab (IDR 20,000–30,000 / \$1.50–\$2.50)
- Or hop on TransJogja (Line 2B), get off near Taman Sari, and walk a bit

Kampung Lawasan

Location: Sleman, with rice fields nearby

Price: From IDR 650,000 (\~\$43) per night

Why you'll Love It: Feels like staying in a countryside villa, complete with a pool, tropical gardens, and home-cooked food. Perfect for people who want nature and comfort in one.

How to get there

- Around 25 minutes from the city by Grab (IDR 30,000–50,000 / \$2–\$3.50)

Alamkita Eco-Village

Location: Imogiri

Price: From IDR 550,000 (\~\$36) per night

Why you'll Love It: This place runs on love, not Wi-Fi. Handmade huts, fresh meals, and starry nights. A lovely reset button for your soul.

How to get there

- About 45 minutes by Grab from the city (IDR 50,000–70,000 / \$3.50–\$5)
- No need to rush—bring a book and enjoy the breeze.

Borobudur Balkondes

Location: Villages around Borobudur

Price: From IDR 400,000 (\~\$26) per night

Why you'll Love It: Run by locals, these cottages let you experience village life while being just minutes from one of the world's greatest temples. Magical at sunrise.

<u>How to get there</u>

- 1.5–2 hours from Yogyakarta by Grab/private car (IDR 300,000–500,000 / \$20–\$35)
- Stay two nights if you can—it's too special to rush.

Why These Stays Make the Trip More Memorable

- You get authentic stories, not just room service
- Locals run most of them—your money helps real families
- They're ideal for mindful travelers, culture lovers, and couples
- Many offer extras like batik lessons, cooking classes, or bike tours
- You'll take better photos—and better memories—home with you

TOP ATTRACTIONS & MUST-SEE SITES

Borobudur Temple

Why You Just Can't Miss It

Let's be honest — some places leave you speechless, and Borobudur is one of them. Imagine this: it's still dark, the air is cool, and you're quietly climbing ancient stone steps by flashlight. Then, as the first light touches the sky, you're standing on top of the world — or so it feels — with mist curling over green jungles and volcanoes in the distance. There's silence, stillness, and then it hits you... this is one of those once-in-a-lifetime travel moments. If you only do one thing in Yogyakarta, make it this.

What to See & Do

- Catch sunrise from the top, it's a calm, spiritual experience that stays with you forever.
- Walk past hundreds of intricate relief carvings and statues that tell centuries of Buddhist stories.
- Find a quiet corner and just sit — locals say the temple's energy is grounding.
- Swing by the on-site museum to deepen your appreciation (yes, even if you're not a history buff!).

Opening Hours & Ticket Info

Sunrise Access (via Manohara Hotel entrance)

- Starts at 4:30 AM
- Around IDR 500,000–600,000 (\~\$32–\$39 USD)

Regular Hours: 6:30 AM–5:00 PM

Adult: IDR 375,000 (\~\$24 USD)

Child: IDR 225,000 (\~\$14 USD)

Heads-up: Access to the top stupa is limited and must be booked ahead — they only allow a certain number of people per day.

How to Get There

Location: Borobudur, Magelang — about 1.5 hours (40 km) from Yogyakarta.

Private Car/Driver

Costs: IDR 500,000–700,000/day (\~\$32–\$45).

Group Tour

Sunrise tours from your hotel cost about IDR 450,000–600,000 (\~\$30–\$40) including transport and ticket.

Public Bus

Cheapest but trickiest. Take TransJogja to Jombor Terminal, then switch to a local bus.

Total cost: around IDR 35,000–50,000 / \~\$2.50–\$3.50. Not ideal for sunrise trips!

Pro Tips for a Magical Visit

Bring a light jacket: It can get chilly before the sun comes up.

Wear comfortable shoes: Those temple steps are no joke.

Don't forget your camera or phone: This is your Instagram moment.

Grab some hot tea and breakfast after: Most sunrise tours include it, or find a cozy café nearby.

Prambanan Temple

If temples could talk, Prambanan would speak in poetry. Towering above the Central Javanese plains, this 9th-century Hindu temple complex isn't just a historical site — it's a spiritual experience.

The moment you walk in, the smell of incense, the sound of wind through ancient stone, and the sheer height of the temple spires hit you all at once. It feels like you've stepped into another world — and honestly, it's hard not to be moved.

Why You'll Love It

Prambanan isn't just beautiful — it's alive with stories. Every wall is carved with tales from the Ramayana, a classic Hindu epic full of romance, war, betrayal, and redemption. It's like reading a graphic novel in stone. And when you stand under the main temple of Shiva the Destroyer, you feel small in the most awe-inspiring way.

This isn't a stop you rush through. This is one to walk slowly... to take in... to remember.

What to Do There

- Explore the main temples dedicated to Shiva, Vishnu, and Brahma — the holy trinity of Hindu gods.
- Walk around the carved reliefs, and let the story of the Ramayana unfold with every step.
- Visit the smaller, quieter shrines — they're photogenic and perfect for peaceful moments.
- Catch a sunset ballet performance of the Ramayana (on select nights). Dancers move like they're floating, with the temple glowing in the background. Magical doesn't even begin to describe it.

Opening Hours & Entry Prices

Open Daily: 6:30 AM – 5:00 PM

Foreign Visitor Tickets

Adults: IDR 375,000 (\~\$24)

Children: IDR 225,000 (\~\$14)

Combo Ticket with Borobudur: IDR 700,000 (\~\$45) – highly recommended if you plan to do both.

Tip: Bring your passport or a copy for ticket validation.

How to Get There

Location: Bokoharjo, Sleman Regency – around 45 minutes (17 km) from downtown Yogyakarta.

By Private Car/Driver: Most convenient and comfortable. A full-day ride usually costs IDR 400,000–600,000 (\~\$26–\$39).

By TransJogja Bus: Take Route 1A. Fare is just IDR 3,500 (\~\$0.25). From the Prambanan terminal, it's a 5–10 minute walk to the gate.

By Motorbike: If you're up for a little adventure, renting a motorbike is fun and budget-friendly at IDR 80,000–100,000/day (\~\$5–\$7).

Don't Leave Without Experiencing This

Sunset Views: The late afternoon light turns the stones gold. It's breathtaking — and less crowded.

Ramayana Ballet (Optional): Live music, vibrant costumes, and the ancient tale told through Javanese dance — all performed with Prambanan as the backdrop.

Tickets start around IDR 150,000 (\~\$10). Well worth it.

Quick Tips

- It gets hot — wear a hat, bring sunscreen, and stay hydrated.
- You can rent a sarong at the entrance (if needed) — respectful dress is appreciated.
- Vendors near the exit sell cute batik scarves and local snacks.
- Take your time. Some places are just meant to be savored — and Prambanan is one of them.

The Sultan's Palace (Kraton)

Why You Really Shouldn't Skip

If you want to feel the heartbeat of Yogyakarta, this is where you go. The Kraton isn't just a beautiful palace—it's the living, breathing soul of the city.

The current Sultan and his family still live here, and the traditions of the past are very much alive today. You're not walking through a

dusty museum—you're stepping into a cultural treasure where history still unfolds in real time. This is the place where you finally "get" what Yogyakarta is all about.

This is one of those places that's not just a stop on your itinerary—it's where the spirit of the city speaks to you. Don't miss it.

What You'll See & Experience

Royal Courtyards & Halls

Wander through grand, open-air pavilions filled with royal heirlooms, carvings, and age-old architecture that feels timeless.

Traditional Performances

If you time your visit right, you can catch gamelan music, wayang kulit (shadow puppet shows), or classical Javanese dance right inside the palace complex.

Mini Museums

placed around the grounds are quiet galleries with photos, sultan memorabilia, batik fabrics, and more that tell the story of Yogyakarta's royal legacy.

Opening Hours & Tickets

Open: Tuesday to Sunday, 8:30 AM – 3:00 PM (last ticket at 2:00 PM)

Closed: Mondays

Entrance Fee: IDR 25,000 for foreign tourists (\~\$1.60 USD)

Note: There's a small additional fee if you want to take photos inside.

How to Get There

Location: Jl. Rotowijayan No. 1, Kraton, Yogyakarta (Right in the city center—very easy to find!)

By Becak (Pedicab): A fun and traditional way to arrive—expect to pay around IDR 20,000–30,000 from Malioboro.

By Taxi or Ride-Hailing App (like Grab or Gojek): Super convenient and affordable—usually around IDR 15,000–25,000 depending on where you're coming from.

Helpful Tips Before You Go

Dress modestly: This is still an active royal residence, so shoulders and knees should be covered.

Guided tours are worth it: For just a little more, a local guide can explain the deeper meaning behind what you're seeing.

Respect the quiet zones: Some parts of the palace are still private and used by the royal family.

Taman Sari Water Castle

Why You Shouldn't Miss It

Taman Sari isn't just a historical site—it's a quiet dream woven into the backstreets of Yogyakarta. Picture this: sunlit stone pathways, hidden doorways, and pools that shimmer like glass in the morning light. This was once the Sultan's private retreat—a royal spa, garden, and secret hideout all in one.

And even though centuries have passed, the magic still lingers.

It's peaceful, mysterious, and deeply beautiful. Honestly? It feels like you're walking through the pages of a forgotten fairytale.

What to See & Do

Royal Bathing Pools

These are the heart of Taman Sari. Deep blue waters, elegant archways, and an old tower where the Sultan once watched over the baths. It's one of the most photogenic spots in all of Yogyakarta.

Underground Mosque

This circular structure with staircases leading into its center is both eerie and calming. People often sit here to rest and soak in the quiet.

Hidden Tunnels

Built for escape and secrecy, many of these tunnels are still intact. Walking through them is like discovering another world.

Artisan Streets Nearby

Just outside the Water Castle, you'll find local artists crafting batik, wood carvings, and silver jewelry. It's the perfect place to buy something meaningful—directly from the maker.

Opening Hours & Ticket Info

Open: Every day, 9:00 AM – 3:00 PM

Entrance: IDR 15,000 (\~\$1 USD)

Camera Fee: IDR 2,000 (\~10 cents) – well worth it!

How to Get There

Location: Jl. Taman, Kraton, Yogyakarta (very close to the Sultan's Palace)

On Foot: From the Kraton, it's an easy 10-minute walk through charming neighborhoods.

By Becak (Pedicab): A breezy ride from Malioboro or Kraton costs around IDR 20,000.

Ride Apps: GoJek or Grab will get you there for about IDR 10,000–20,000 depending on traffic.

Local Tips

Wear comfy shoes: The cobbled paths and steps can be tricky, especially if it rains.

Come early or late: Beat the heat and the crowds. Morning light is perfect for photos.

Talk to a local guide: For just IDR 50,000–75,000, you can hear the hidden stories and symbolism behind each building. It really brings the place to life.

Mount Merapi & Jeep Adventure Tours

Why You Shouldn't Miss It

Ever wanted to ride through a volcanic landscape like you're in an action movie? Welcome to Mount Merapi — Indonesia's most active volcano and one of Yogyakarta's most thrilling experiences.

This isn't just a mountain; it's a living, breathing force of nature. Locals call it the "Mountain of Fire," and once you see it up close, you'll understand why.

The best way to explore its dramatic terrain? A bumpy, dusty, exhilarating 4x4 jeep ride that takes you straight into the heart of it all. Between ash-covered valleys, lava boulders, and haunting ruins, this tour offers both adventure and emotional insight into how people here live side by side with the volcano.

What to See & Do

Lava Tour by Jeep

Hold on tight! These rugged jeeps (driven by experienced locals) take you through the blackened landscape left by Merapi's past eruptions. You'll bounce through riverbeds, off-road paths, and even stop at old villages buried in ash. It's both thrilling and humbling.

Museum Sisa Hartaku (My Remaining Belongings Museum)

This tiny but powerful museum is set inside a house destroyed by the 2010 eruption. Inside, you'll see burned-out motorcycles, clocks frozen in time, and melted household items — a raw, personal glimpse into disaster survival.

Bunker Kaliadem

Built as a refuge during eruptions, this underground bunker is now a stop on most tours. It's a little eerie, a little fascinating, and adds another layer to the Merapi story.

Sunrise or Sunset Tours

Want that Instagram moment? Take the sunrise tour. Watching the first light hit Merapi's peak is almost spiritual — calm, golden, and unforgettable. Sunset's not bad either!

Ticket Info & Jeep Tour Prices (as of 2025)

Short Tour (1 hour): IDR 350,000 (\~USD \$22)

Medium Tour (1.5–2 hours): IDR 450,000

Long Tour (2.5–3 hours): IDR 600,000+

Price is per jeep (not per person) and each jeep fits up to 4 people, so bring friends or share to save.

How to Get There

Starting Point: Most tours begin from the Kaliurang area, around 25 km north of Yogyakarta.

By Ride-Hailing App (Grab/GoCar): Around IDR 80,000–100,000 from the city center.

By Scooter: If you're confident on the road, renting a scooter (IDR 75,000–100,000/day) gives you flexibility — but drive with care.

Local Tips

Wear closed shoes: It's rocky and dusty out there.

Bring a jacket: The mountain air is cool, especially at sunrise.

Hang onto your phone/camera: Those bumps are real!

Listen to your guide: Many are locals who've lived through the eruptions and have powerful stories to share.

Cash only: Most places here don't take cards, so come prepared.

Mount Merapi isn't just a tourist spot. It's a reminder of nature's power — and the strength of the people who live alongside it. Whether you come for the adventure, the view, or the history, you'll leave with a story worth telling.

Malioboro Street

Why You Shouldn't Miss It

Malioboro isn't just a street — it's an experience. It's the soul of Yogyakarta packed into a few buzzing kilometers. Whether you're a curious first-timer or a returning traveler chasing nostalgia, there's something here that will pull at your heart.

The scent of grilled street food, the sound of buskers strumming guitars, the colorful batik fabrics fluttering in the breeze — it's where every corner tells a story, and every night feels like a festival.

Malioboro isn't just where you go — it's where you feel. Whether you're sipping sweet tea at a roadside stall or chatting with a vendor about how long it took to make that batik shawl, you'll find joy in the simplest things here. It's where Yogyakarta truly opens its arms.

What to See & Do

Batik & Bargains

This is souvenir heaven. You'll find beautiful hand-painted batik shirts, bags, fans, sarongs — even umbrellas. Don't worry if you're not a pro at bargaining; a smile goes a long way. Vendors are used to tourists and usually open to some friendly negotiation.

Eat Like a Local

If your taste buds love a little adventure, this is your playground. Pull up a plastic stool at a street stall and try satay, bakso (meatball soup), or gudeg (sweet jackfruit stew). Most dishes cost under IDR 20,000 (\~\$1.30), and the flavors are unforgettable. Eating "lesehan-style" — sitting on mats along the sidewalk — is a must-try local tradition.

Soak in the Sounds

In the evening, the street transforms into a casual concert. From acoustic guitars to angklung (bamboo instruments), you'll find music around every bend. Stop and listen for a bit — it's pure joy and adds so much to the atmosphere.

Pasar Beringharjo

Just off Malioboro, this traditional market is a labyrinth of local life. Whether you're hunting for herbs, batik, antiques, or oddities, this is your spot. It's chaotic, colorful, and completely charming.

Opening Hours & Costs

Malioboro Street: Always open — day or night!

Shops & stalls: Usually 9:00 AM – 10:00 PM

Pasar Beringharjo: 8:00 AM – 5:00 PM

Street food snacks: IDR 5,000–20,000

Souvenirs: Batik from IDR 50,000; handmade accessories from IDR 30,000

<u>How to Get There</u>

Location: Central Yogyakarta — just say "Malioboro" to any local, and they'll point the way.

By Becak (Pedicab): A fun, old-school way to arrive. Expect to pay IDR 15,000–30,000 depending on the distance.

By Grab/Taxi: Around IDR 20,000–40,000 from most areas in the city.

By TransJogja Bus: Take Route 1A or 2A — get off at Malioboro stop. Fare: IDR 3,600.

Local Tips

Evenings are golden: Lights twinkle, music fills the air, and everyone's out enjoying the city.

Carry cash: Cards are rarely accepted. Small bills are super handy.

Stay aware: It's safe, but it's still a busy street — keep your bag zipped and close.

Take your time: Don't rush. Wander, eat, shop, sit and people-watch. That's how Malioboro is best enjoyed.

Ullen Sentalu Museum & Cultural Highlights

Why You Shouldn't Miss It

This isn't your average museum. Ullen Sentalu feels like stepping into a quiet sanctuary where Javanese culture whispers its secrets to you. Located in the misty foothills of Mount Merapi, it's cool, peaceful, and beautifully mysterious. If you want to feel Javanese history — not just see it behind glass — this place will speak to you.

What You'll Love Doing Here

Meet the Women Behind the Kingdoms

One of the most touching parts? The personal letters, poems, and batik collections of Javanese princesses. You'll hear their voices, their emotions,

their thoughts — and suddenly, history becomes very human.

Stroll Through Hidden Gardens

Between the museum rooms are quiet garden paths with sculptures, fountains, and the smell of fresh mountain air. It's the kind of place where you slow down without even trying.

Take the Guided Tour (You'll Be Glad You Did)

You can't wander alone here — but that's actually what makes it special. The museum provides a guide (included in the ticket), and they're really good at making each room feel like a story unfolding. No boring facts — just real connections.

Opening Hours & Prices

Open: Tuesday to Sunday, 8:30 AM – 4:00 PM

Closed: On Mondays

Entrance Fee

Foreign visitors: IDR 100,000

Local visitors: IDR 50,000

Free tour included (English or Bahasa)

Where It Is & How to Get There

Location: Jalan Boyong KM 25, Kaliurang — about 40 minutes north of the city

By Ride-Hailing App or Taxi: Around IDR 80,000–100,000 from central Yogyakarta

By Scooter: Perfect if you're up for a scenic ride through mountain villages (rentals from IDR 70,000/day)

By Public Bus: Take a TransJogja bus towards Kaliurang, then grab a short ojek ride to the entrance

Helpful Tips from Locals

Bring a light sweater: It's much cooler up here

No indoor photography: But the outdoor spaces are totally photo-worthy

Go in the morning if you want to avoid the crowd and enjoy the calm

Stop by a café nearby after your visit: The area has charming little spots with coffee and mountain views

Final Thought

Ullen Sentalu isn't flashy. It's gentle, quiet, and soulful — and maybe that's what makes it so unforgettable. You don't just learn about Javanese culture here... you feel it. Slow down, take it all in, and let the spirit of Java sink in a little deeper.

HIDDEN GEMS

Jomblang Cave

Why You Shouldn't Miss It

If you've ever wanted to feel like you've stepped into another world, Jomblang Cave is the place.

Picture this, you're lowered slowly into a massive sinkhole, and as your feet touch the forest floor below, it's dark, damp, and silent. Then, just when you think it can't get any more surreal, a beam of sunlight pours through a hole 60 meters above your head — the famous "heavenly light." It's one of those once-in-a-lifetime experiences that you'll talk about for years.

What You'll Do Down There

Be Lowered into the Earth

No experience needed. You'll be safely strapped into a harness and guided down by professionals who do this every day.

Explore an Underground Forest

Yes, a real forest under the surface — mossy, misty, and a bit eerie in the best way.

Catch the Light Beam

From 10:00 AM to around noon, that magical sunlight beams in. It's like nature turned on a spotlight just for you.

Trek to Grubug Cave

You'll walk (or sometimes slide) through the mud to a deeper chamber where you can hear an underground river echoing in the dark. It's haunting and beautiful.

How to Get There

Location: Jetis Wetan, Pacarejo Village, Gunung Kidul Regency

Distance from Yogyakarta: About 1.5 to 2 hours by car

Best Ways to Go

Hire a Private Driver: Most comfortable, especially if you're not used to winding roads — expect to pay around IDR 500,000–700,000 round trip.

Rent a Scooter: If you're adventurous and confident, scooters go for about IDR 70,000/day.

Join a Tour: Easy and often includes lunch, gear, and transport — usually around IDR 450,000–600,000/person.

Cost & What's Included

Cave Entry: IDR 500,000 per person

Includes full safety gear: helmet, boots, harness, guides, and transport into the cave

Limited slots per day: It's smart to book ahead, especially during weekends or high season

What to Bring & Know

Wear Old Clothes: You will get muddy — and it's part of the fun.

Bring Extra Clothes & Towel: There are rinse-off stations, but nothing fancy.

Protect Your Phone/Camera: The cave's damp, so waterproof bags or covers are lifesavers.

Get There Early: Arrive before 9:00 AM to make sure you catch the light show — it doesn't last all day!

Practical information

It's muddy, it's messy, it's a little scary at first — and it's absolutely unforgettable. If there's one place in Yogyakarta that feels like an adventure movie come to life, it's this. Don't leave it off your list.

Gunung Kidul's Secret Beaches

Why You Shouldn't Miss It

You know those beaches you dream about when you're stuck in traffic or scrolling through social media at work? The ones with soft white sand, clear blue waves, and zero crowds? That's Gunung Kidul.

Just a couple of hours south of Yogyakarta, this coastal region is full of hidden gems—unspoiled beaches where you can stretch out, breathe in the sea breeze, and feel like you've got the whole ocean to yourself.

If you're craving a break from temples and city life, this is where you go to slow down, snack on grilled fish, and maybe even fall asleep under a palm tree.

Beaches You'll Want to Keep a Secret (But Won't)

Indrayanti Beach

One of the more developed ones, but still laid-back. You'll find little beachside cafés, good swimming, and fresh coconuts. Great for first-timers.

Pok Tunggal Beach

Quiet, charming, and flanked by tall cliffs. Bring your camera — the sunset here is the kind that makes you feel all warm inside.

Wediombo Beach

A little more rugged, with natural rock pools that appear when the tide is low. Also a fun spot for beginner surfers or just dipping your feet

Timang Beach

Feeling brave? Ride a DIY-style gondola across crashing waves to a tiny offshore island. It's wild, unforgettable, and definitely not your average beach day.

How to Get There

Location: Gunung Kidul Regency, about 2–3 hours south of Yogyakarta

Private Driver: Super comfy for groups or families — expect to pay IDR 600,000–750,000 for a full day

Scooter Rental: If you're confident on two wheels, rent one for IDR 70,000–100,000/day and enjoy the freedom

Tour Packages: These usually cover a few beaches and meals, priced around IDR 400,000–600,000 per person

What to Pack

Sunscreen and a hat: The sun doesn't play around here

Snacks and water: Some beaches don't have shops

A camera or even a drone: Trust me, you'll want to show these views off

Sandals or water shoes: Some beaches have sharp rocks

Extra Tips

- Try to go early in the morning or just before sunset — less heat, better light, fewer people
- Some beaches don't have facilities, so bring a towel, wipes, or even a picnic
- Help keep these beaches beautiful: take all your trash with you
- No showers? That's part of the charm. Just plan to rinse off when you're back in town

Practical information

Gunung Kidul doesn't try to impress you with flashy resorts or wild parties. It wins you over with its calm, its raw beauty, and the sense of stillness you didn't even realize you needed. It's the kind of place that makes you take a deep breath... and feel grateful to be there.

Mangunan Fruit Forest & Viewpoints

Why You Shouldn't Miss It

If you've ever dreamed of standing above the clouds —not in a plane, but with your feet firmly planted on the earth — this is your chance. Mangunan isn't just a place; it's a moment. The kind that makes you stop scrolling, take a breath, and just feel.

Located in the cool highlands of Dlingo, just over an hour from Yogyakarta, this spot is all about soft sunrises, misty mornings, and a peaceful calm that stays with you long after you leave.

And it's not just about the views. This is a working fruit forest where nature feels alive. Depending on the season, you'll walk past rows of guava trees, jackfruit hanging low, and even the occasional durian — all part of the experience.

What You'll Love Doing

Catch the Sunrise

This is the main event. Arrive early — like, pre-coffee early — and you'll be rewarded with an ocean of mist rolling through the valley. It's surreal, like nature's version of a dream sequence.

Snap a Photo

Treehouses, cliffside decks, bamboo swings — it's a photo-lover's paradise. Even if you're not big on selfies, the views might convince you otherwise.

Wander the Fruit Forest

Depending on the season, you might be able to sample fruit fresh from the trees. Ask one of the friendly local caretakers — they'll likely offer you something sweet with a smile.

Explore Nearby Hills

Don't stop at just one view. Nearby Bukit Panguk, Becici Peak, and Watu Goyang offer their own slice of magic — and they're all within a short drive.

Getting There

Location: Mangunan, Dlingo District — about 1 to 1.5 hours by car or scooter from Yogyakarta

By Car or Driver: Great for groups or families — expect around IDR 400,000–500,000 for a day trip

By Scooter: Perfect for solo travelers or adventurous duos — around IDR 70,000–100,000/day

Entry Fee: Super affordable — just IDR 5,000–10,000 (a few thousand extra if you're using a DSLR camera)

Parking: Yes — easy and safe

When to Visit

Early morning is best: Arrive before 6:00 AM for the mist show

(April–October): Offers clearer skies and brighter views

What to Pack

A warm layer: It can get pretty chilly before sunrise

Snacks and water: There are a few small stalls, but better safe than snackless

A fully charged camera or phone: Trust us, you'll want to remember this

Shoes with grip: Trails can get slick after rain

Little Things That Make It Special

- You might hear birdsong while sipping tea from a roadside stall.
- Locals will often greet you with a nod or "pagi!" (good morning).
- There's something about watching the clouds roll through a valley that makes all your problems feel smaller.

Practical information

Mangunan is a reminder that sometimes the best parts of a trip are the quiet ones. No crowds, no chaos —just you, the hills, and a sky that slowly turns gold. It's not a bucket list stop. It's better than that. It's a memory waiting to happen.

Traditional Villages & Local Markets

Why You Shouldn't Miss It

Sometimes, it's not the big landmarks that stick with you — it's the little moments. A smile from a village elder. The scent of freshly fried banana fritters. The quiet rustle of wind through rice fields.

If you want to feel Yogyakarta, not just see it, this is where the magic lives.

Venturing into the villages and markets around the city offers a rare, intimate look into daily life. People still live by age-old customs, making things by hand, cooking with recipes passed down for generations, and greeting strangers like long-lost friends. It's not a show for tourists — it's just life, beautiful and unscripted.

Where to Go

Kotagede

Silverwork, Serenity & Stories

Once the capital of an ancient kingdom, today Kotagede is a peaceful neighborhood filled with narrow alleys, old teak houses, and some of the best silversmiths in the country.

What's special: Watch skilled artisans shape silver into beautiful jewelry, walk through a royal cemetery wrapped in mystery and incense, and explore the quiet charm of a place that seems paused in time.

How to get there: Just 30 minutes from the city center by taxi or scooter (\~IDR 30,000–50,000).

Cost: Free to explore. Some small donation fees for the royal tombs or museums.

Kasongan Village

Where Clay Becomes Art

This one's for the creatives. Just 12 km from the city, Kasongan is a vibrant village where nearly every home doubles as a pottery studio.

What's special: Take a pottery class, talk with local artists, and browse everything from tiny trinkets to massive garden sculptures.

How to get there: Around IDR 60,000–100,000 by scooter or taxi, round trip.

Cost: Free to enter the village. Workshops start from around IDR 50,000.

Tembi Cultural Village

Rural Bliss & Tradition

Think open skies, rice paddies, and traditional Javanese houses with breezy porches and birdsong in the background. Tembi is peaceful, welcoming, and full of culture.

What's special: Visit the Tembi House of Culture, try local dishes, and stay in a joglo-style homestay for a night of real Javanese hospitality.

How to get there: 20–30 minutes by car or scooter (\~IDR 40,000–60,000).

Cost: Free entrance, small fee for the museum. Accommodations vary depending on season and amenities.

Markets You'll Love

Pasar Beringharjo

The Grand Dame of Yogyakarta Markets

Right in the heart of Malioboro Street, this place is buzzing with life. If you're into textiles, spices, antiques, or just people-watching — this is your spot.

Top finds: Batik (from hand-dyed masterpieces to fun printed T-shirts), traditional snacks, herbal medicine, and souvenirs galore.

Open: Daily, 8:00 AM – 4:00 PM

Tip: Go early to beat the heat and crowds. Bring cash and your best bargaining smile.

Getting there: Walkable from many city hotels or a short becak ride (\~IDR 20,000–30,000).

Pasar Prawirotaman

Local Vibes Only

Smaller and more relaxed, this market near the backpacker hub of Prawirotaman is perfect if you want to escape the tourist buzz.

Top finds: Morning fruits, fresh vegetables, hot jadah tempeh (sticky rice with sweet soy-glazed tempeh), and ginger tea straight from the pot.

Open: Early morning until about noon.

Good to know: It's perfect for a quick local breakfast before starting your day's adventures.

Tips

Start Early: Villages and markets come alive at sunrise. By late morning, the best goodies are gone — and the sun gets pretty intense.

Be Respectful: Smile, greet people politely with a "selamat pagi," and ask before taking photos. You'll be amazed how many stories open up just from being kind.

Bring Small Bills: Most local vendors don't have change for big notes. Cash is king — especially small denominations (IDR 2,000–10,000).

Embrace the Slow: Don't rush. Wander. Watch. Talk. Taste. These moments — the slow ones — are what you'll remember.

Silent Temples, Hilltop Sunrises & Forgotten Trails

There's something magical about getting away from it all — no crowds, no rush, just you, nature, and history quietly resting in the hills. These aren't the places printed on postcards, but they're the ones that stick with you long after the trip ends. Yogyakarta's hidden hills and ancient sanctuaries are where you'll find peace, perspective, and maybe even a little piece of yourself.

Candi Abang

The Temple Covered in Grass, Wrapped in Mystery

Location: Jogotirto, Berbah, Sleman Regency

Imagine this: a wide grassy mound, like something out of a fantasy novel — and beneath it? A centuries-old Hindu temple built from red bricks. There are no fences or ticket booths here. Just open sky, birdsong, and that quiet feeling that maybe, just maybe, you're standing on forgotten ground.

Best Time to Go: Sunrise or golden hour — the lighting is surreal.

Cost: Free

How to Get There: Around 45 minutes from the city center. You can rent a scooter or take a ride-hailing car (around IDR 50,000–80,000 one way).

Tip: Come with your favorite playlist or in silence —both suit the mood.

Candi Ijo

The Temple with the Sky for a Roof

Location: Sambirejo, Prambanan, Sleman Regency

This is the highest temple in Yogyakarta, sitting peacefully above the clouds — or at least it feels that way. It's not as famous as Prambanan, which means you might have the whole place nearby. The view? Simply breathtaking. You can spot the runway at the airport, the sprawling city below, and mountains in the distance.

Best Time to Go: Just before sunset — it's cinematic.

Entrance Fee: IDR 10,000

How to Get There: Near Ratu Boko, about 45 minutes from the city. Use Grab, Gojek, or rent a bike (IDR 60,000–100,000).

Photography Tip: Bring a wide-angle lens — trust us on this.

Punthuk Setumbu

Mist, Magic, and Borobudur from Afar

Location: Karangrejo, Borobudur, Magelang

You've seen Borobudur up close — but have you seen it floating above the jungle in the early morning mist? That's the view from Punthuk Setumbu, and it's nothing short of magical. Fewer tourists, a chill vibe, and a sunrise you'll remember forever.

Best Time to Go: Be there by 4:30 AM — yes, it's early, but so worth it.

Entrance Fee: IDR 20,000

How to Get There: A 45-minute ride from Yogyakarta (around IDR 70,000–100,000 by car or scooter).

Suroloyo Peak

Where the Sky Feels Closer

Location: Gerbosari, Samigaluh, Kulon Progo

Located in the Menoreh Hills, this peak isn't just the highest around — it's also the most spiritual. Local legends say it's where gods used to meditate. Climb the 200+ steps and you'll understand why. On clear days, you can see not one, but four volcanoes in the distance. It's powerful, peaceful, and worth every step.

Best Time to Go: Early morning or just before sunset.

Entrance Fee: Donation-based (bring small cash).

How to Get There: About 40 km from the city —best with your own ride or a local driver.

Final Thoughts & Local Wisdom

These places don't ask for much — just your time, your curiosity, and your willingness to slow down. There are no queues, no loudspeakers, and no vendors pushing souvenirs. What you'll find instead are still winds, old stones, open skies, and a deep sense of being right where you're supposed to be.

Don't forget

- Pack water, a light snack, and your favorite tunes.
- Save your map offline — reception gets shaky.
- Say hello to locals. They're kind and might share a story or shortcut you won't find online.
- Take your time. These aren't "see it and go" places. They're "sit, breathe, and feel something" places.

ITINERARIES FOR EVERY TRAVELER

1-Day Highlights Tour

Short on time? No worries — you can still soak in the magic of Yogyakarta in just one incredible day. This itinerary is for those who want to experience the city's spiritual roots, royal charm, and vibrant street life, all without feeling like they're in a race. It's fast-paced but doable — and every moment is worth it.

Morning

Sunrise Magic at Borobudur

Your day starts before the sun even thinks about rising. Set your alarm for around 3:30–4:00 AM — yep, it's early, but this is one of those moments that makes the whole trip worth it.

Catch a sunrise tour at Borobudur Temple, the largest Buddhist monument in the world.

Picture this: misty hills, ancient stupas, and the first light of day breaking over the horizon — it's spiritual, peaceful, and jaw-droppingly beautiful.

Location: Magelang (about 1 hour 15 minutes from central Yogyakarta)

Cost: Sunrise ticket from IDR 500,000 (for foreign visitors)

How to get there

Private car hire: (around IDR 450,000 for the day) is the most flexible option.

Or, join a group sunrise tour, usually IDR 650,000–800,000, including hotel pickup, transport, and a guide.

Quick Tip: After sunrise, grab a hot coffee and a light local breakfast at a nearby warung or the café by the temple — trust us, coffee tastes better when you've watched it rise with the sun.

Late Morning

The Royal Heart – Kraton & Taman Sari

Once you're back in Yogyakarta (usually around 9:30–10:00 AM), it's time to dive into the city's regal history.

Kraton (Sultan's Palace)

Step into living history — the Kraton is not just a museum; it's the actual home of the Sultan. Stroll through elegant courtyards, check out royal heirlooms, and if you're lucky, catch a traditional Javanese performance before noon.

Location: Jl. Rotowijayan Blok No. 1

Entrance: IDR 25,000

Suggested Time: 1–1.5 hours

Getting there

From your hotel or drop-off point in the city, take a Grab ride (app-based taxi, cheap and reliable) or hop in a becak (pedicab) for a fun, local experience.

Taman Sari Water Castle

Just a short walk or ride from Kraton, this enchanting ruin was once the Sultan's private garden and bathing complex. It's full of photogenic spots — arched tunnels, serene pools, and stories of hidden passages.

Location: Jl. Taman, Kraton

Entrance: IDR 15,000

Suggested Time: 1 hour

Hire a local guide at the gate for IDR 50,000. They know the coolest stories and secret photo spots.

Lunch

Taste of Yogyakarta at Gudeg Yu Djum

Time to eat like a local! Head over to Gudeg Yu Djum, a legendary spot to try gudeg — Yogyakarta's signature sweet jackfruit stew. It comes with rice, boiled egg, and tender chicken — comforting, delicious, and totally authentic.

Location: Jl. Wijilan No.167 (just a few minutes from Taman Sari)

Cost: Around IDR 30,000–50,000 per person

<u>Getting there</u>

Easily walkable from Taman Sari (10–15 minutes), or hop on a becak if your legs need a break.

Afternoon

Malioboro Street – Souvenirs & Street Scenes

No trip to Yogyakarta is complete without a stroll down Malioboro Street. It's the beating heart of the city — lively, a little chaotic, and filled with colorful market stalls, batik shops, and street food carts. It's the perfect spot to pick up souvenirs, snap some street photos, and soak in local life.

Location: Jl. Malioboro, central city

Cost: Free to explore, budget IDR 100,000–200,000 if you're shopping

Getting there

A Grab ride from Gudeg Yu Djum will take about 10 minutes, or go old-school and flag a becak.

Try This: Grab a cup of es dawet (sweet coconut and palm sugar drink) from a street vendor. It's refreshing, especially in the heat.

Evening Options

Choose Your Own Adventure

You've got two fantastic ways to wrap up your day —one for thrill-seekers, the other for culture lovers.

Option 1: Mount Merapi Jeep Adventure

Still got energy? Buckle up for a jeep tour around Mount MerapiIndonesia's most active volcano. You'll ride through lava-scarred villages, old bunkers, and rugged landscapes. It's dramatic and a bit wild — perfect for an adrenaline kick.

Starting Point: Kaliurang area (1–1.5 hours north of the city)

Cost: IDR 350,000–500,000 per jeep (shared by 2–3 people)

Time: Tours run from 4:30 PM – 6:30 PM

How to get there

Arrange transport with your driver from earlier, or book a combined tour through a local travel agency or online app like Traveloka or Klook.

Option 2: Ramayana Ballet at Prambanan

Prefer something poetic to end your day? Catch the Ramayana Ballet — a spellbinding performance of dance, fire, and myth set against the backdrop of Prambanan Temple. It's a stunning mix of history and artistry.

Location: Prambanan Temple

Tickets: From IDR 150,000 (standard) to IDR 500,000 (VIP)

Time: 7:30 PM – 9:30 PM (seasonal, check in advance)

How to get there

About 45–60 minutes by car from central Yogyakarta. Book a round-trip Grab ride or join a tour that includes transport.

Nightcap & Chill

Winding Down

After an action-packed day, treat yourself to a relaxed evening drink or snack.

Head to ViaVia Café in Prawirotaman for a cozy atmosphere and travel vibes.

Or wander Sosrowijayan Street near Malioboro for cheap eats and backpacker bars.

Whatever you choose, take a moment to just breathe it all in — the sounds, the smells, the soul of Yogyakarta.

3-Day Culture & Food Journey

A trip for travelers who love storytelling, flavors, and soulful connections.

Day 1 (Where the Past Lives On)

Start with a Sunrise at Borobudur

Wake up very early — we're talking 3:30 AM early — but trust me, it's worth it. The drive to Borobudur, the world's largest Buddhist temple, takes about 90 minutes from the city, but as the mist lifts over the ancient stone carvings and golden light washes across the horizon, you'll forget about the alarm clock.

Location: Borobudur, Magelang

Go by: Private driver, Grab, or tour package (most hotels can arrange it)

Entrance (sunrise access): around IDR 500,000

Brunch Like a Local at Pasar Kranggan

By the time you're back in Yogyakarta, you're going to be hungry. Head to Pasar Kranggan, a bustling market near the famous Tugu monument. It's full of street-side stalls sizzling with local eats. Try serabi (rice pancakes) or a humble cup of kopi joss — a coffee with burning charcoal in it (yes, really!).

Location: Near Tugu Jogja, Central City

Get there by: Becak or Grab (IDR 10,000–20,000)

Snacks: IDR 5,000–20,000

Midday at the Kraton & Taman Sari

After brunch, stroll over to the Kraton, the Sultan's Palace — it's the living, breathing heart of Yogyakarta. Right nearby is Taman Sari, once a royal bathing complex, now a dreamy maze of ruins and hidden pools.

Location: Central Yogyakarta

Walk or take a becak from Malioboro

Kraton: IDR 15,000

Taman Sari: IDR 15,000

Guide (optional): IDR 50,000

Afternoon Workshop & Lunch at ViaVia

Next, head to the hip neighborhood of Prawirotaman. At ViaVia Café, you can eat, relax, and also join a hands-on workshop — like batik painting or silver jewelry making. It's a creative way to experience Yogyakarta's artisan spirit.

Location: Prawirotaman

Take a Grab or taxi (\~IDR 20,000 from city center)

Workshop: IDR 150,000–250,000

Lunch: IDR 50,000–75,000

Evening Stroll Down Malioboro Street

End your day on MalioboroYogyakarta's famous shopping street. It comes alive at night — buskers, batik sellers, and rows of angkringan (street food carts). Grab a plastic stool, order nasi kucing and wedang ronde, and just soak it all in.

Location: Malioboro Street, Central City

Walk or ride a becak

Dinner: IDR 20,000–40,000

Day 2 (Temples, Legends & Golden Hour Views)

Morning at Prambanan & Plaosan Temples

Begin your day at the majestic Prambanan Temple, a towering Hindu masterpiece. Just a short drive away is Plaosan, a peaceful Buddhist complex often overlooked by tourists. Together, they show off Java's deep spiritual roots.

Location: East of the city, \~17 km from center

Take a Grab or book a morning tour

Prambanan: IDR 362,500

Plaosan: IDR 15,000

Lunch with a View at Abhayagiri

Right nearby is Abhayagiri Restaurant, perched on a hill with stunning views of Prambanan and Mount Merapi. It's the kind of place where lunch feels like a ceremony — try the grilled fish or beef rendang.

Location: Bukit Sumberwatu, near Ratu Boko

5–10 mins from Prambanan

Dishes range: IDR 75,000–150,000

Sunset at Ratu Boko Palace

Just before sunset, head up to Ratu Boko Palace —ancient ruins on a hilltop. The sun sets behind distant volcanoes and temple silhouettes, and it's one of those moments that feels completely timeless.

Location: Close to Prambanan

Same area as lunch

Entrance: IDR 150,000 (or combo ticket with Prambanan: IDR 552,000)

Evening

Ramayana Ballet or Nightcap in Town

If you're up for it, catch the Ramayana Ballet — a traditional Javanese performance held right in front of Prambanan under the stars (check schedule in advance).

Location: Prambanan Open-Air Theatre

Tickets: IDR 150,000–500,000

Or head back to Prawirotaman and grab a drink at Sae Café — laid-back, cozy, and full of fellow travelers sharing stories.

Day 3 (Villages, Nature, and Javanese Flavors)

Morning in a Local Village

Trade the city for the countryside. Book a half-day visit to Candirejo (near Borobudur) or Pentingsari (near Mount Merapi). You'll ride in ox carts, try making tofu, play gamelan, or pick herbs for jamu (traditional drinks). It's authentic, personal, and heartwarming.

Location: Candirejo (Magelang) or Pentingsari (Merapi foothills)

Usually includes hotel pickup with a tour

Village experience: IDR 250,000–400,000 (often includes lunch)

Lunch

Home-Cooked & Shared on Banana Leaves

Your lunch will likely be part of the village visit — a simple yet unforgettable spread of rice, vegetables, tempeh, sambal, and warm tea, served by your local hosts.

Included in the village tour

Afternoon

Lava Jeep Adventure at Mount Merapi

Cap off your trip with a blast — literally. Take a lava jeep tour through old eruption sites of Mount Merapi. You'll visit lava-damaged villages, bunkers, and see how resilient this land and its people really are.

Location: Kaliadem, north of Yogyakarta

Most tours include pickup or you can drive there (\~1 hr)

Jeep tour: IDR 350,000–500,000 per jeep (up to 4 people)

Dinner Like Royalty at Bale Raos

For your final dinner, treat yourself to Bale Raos, the only restaurant that serves dishes from the Sultan's family recipe book. It's classy, quiet, and a lovely way to close out your time here.

Location: Next to Kraton, Central City

Take a Grab or taxi from your hotel

Main courses: IDR 75,000–150,000

5-Day Balanced Adventure

Day 1: (Arrival and Cultural submersion)

Morning

Arrival in Yogyakarta

Touching down at Yogyakarta International Airport (YIA), the warm, humid air greets you like an old friend.

How to Get There

Fly into YIA. From the airport, taxis and ride-hailing services are readily available to take you to your accommodation in the city center.

Estimated Cost: Taxi fares range from IDR 150,000 to IDR 200,000.

Location: Yogyakarta International Airport, Kulon Progo Regency

Afternoon

Explore the Kraton (Sultan's Palace)

Stepping into the Kraton feels like entering a living museum. The palace's intricate architecture and the soft gamelan music playing in the background transport you to a bygone era.

How to Get There

Located in the city center; easily accessible by taxi or becak (cycle rickshaw).

Estimated Cost: Entrance fee is around IDR 15,000.

Location: Jl. Rotowijayan Blok No. 1, Panembahan, Kraton, Yogyakarta City

Evening

Stroll Along Malioboro Street

As the sun sets, Malioboro Street comes alive with vibrant lights and the aroma of street food. Strolling here, you feel the city's heartbeat.

How to Get There

A short walk or becak ride from the Kraton.

Estimated Cost: Free to explore; shopping and food costs vary.

Location: Jl. Malioboro, Yogyakarta City

Day 2 (Temples and Traditional Arts)

Morning

Visit Borobudur Temple

Witnessing the sunrise over Borobudur is a spiritual experience. The morning mist wraps around the ancient stupas, creating a mystical atmosphere.

How to Get There

Approximately 1.5-hour drive from Yogyakarta; consider hiring a driver or joining a tour.

Estimated Cost: Entrance fee is around IDR 375,000.

Location: Borobudur, Magelang Regency

Afternoon

Explore Mendut and Pawon Temples

These smaller temples offer a peaceful retreat. The serenity here allows for quiet reflection amid ancient stone carvings.

How to Get There

Short drive from Borobudur; often included in temple tours.

Estimated Cost: Combined entrance fee is approximately IDR 10,000.

Location: Mendut and Pawon, Magelang Regency

Evening

Attend the Ramayana Ballet at Prambanan

Under the starlit sky, the Ramayana Ballet unfolds with captivating dances and music, bringing ancient tales to life against the backdrop of Prambanan Temple.

How to Get There

Approximately 30-minute drive from Yogyakarta city center.

Estimated Cost: Ticket prices range from IDR 125,000 to IDR 400,000, depending on seating.

Location: Prambanan Temple Complex, Sleman Regency

Day 3 (Nature and Adventure)

Morning

Mount Merapi Jeep Tour

Feel the thrill as the jeep navigates rugged terrains, offering panoramic views of Mount Merapi's majestic slopes and the surrounding landscapes.

How to Get There

Approximately 1-hour drive from Yogyakarta; tours often include hotel pickup.

Estimated Cost: Jeep tours cost around IDR 350,000 to IDR 500,000 per jeep (up to 4 people).

Location: Mount Merapi, Sleman Regency

Afternoon

Visit Ullen Sentalu Museum

Located in the highlands, this museum offers a deep dive into Javanese culture and art, with exhibits that tell stories of royal families and traditions.

How to Get There

Located near Mount Merapi; accessible by car or as part of a tour.

Estimated Cost: Entrance fee is around IDR 50,000.

Location: Jl. Boyong Km 25, Kaliurang, Sleman Regency

Evening

Dine at The House of Raminten

This quirky restaurant combines traditional Javanese cuisine with an eclectic ambiance, making for a memorable dining experience.

How to Get There

Located in the city center; accessible by taxi or becak.

Estimated Cost: Meals range from IDR 30,000 to IDR 100,000.

Location: Jl. FM Noto No.7, Kotabaru, Yogyakarta City

Day 4 (Caves and Beaches)

Morning

Explore Jomblang Cave

Descending into Jomblang Cave, you're greeted by the ethereal "heaven's light" filtering through the cave's opening—a sight that leaves you in awe.

How to Get There

Approximately 1.5 to 2-hour drive from Yogyakarta; tours are recommended.

Estimated Cost: Tours cost around IDR 500,000, including equipment and guides.

Location: Jetis Wetan, Semanu, Gunungkidul Regency

Afternoon

Visit Timang Beach

Experience the thrill of crossing to a rocky outcrop via a traditional gondola or suspension bridge, with waves crashing below—a true adventure.

How to Get There

Approximately 1-hour drive from Jomblang Cave; often included in adventure tours.

Estimated Cost: Gondola ride costs around IDR 200,000; bridge crossing is about IDR 100,000.

Location: Purwodadi, Tepus, Gunungkidul Regency

Evening

Relax at Indrayanti Beach

Unwind on the sandy shores, enjoy fresh seafood, and watch the sunset paint the sky in hues of orange and pink—a perfect end to an adventurous day.

Short drive from Timang Beach; accessible by car or tour.

Estimated Cost: Entrance fee is around IDR 10,000; food costs vary.

Location: Tepus, Gunungkidul Regency

Day 5 (Art and Farewell)

Morning

Visit Affandi Museum

Explore the works and former residence of Indonesia's renowned painter, Affandi. The museum's unique architecture and art pieces offer a glimpse into the artist's life.

How to Get There

Located along the main road; accessible by taxi or ride-hailing services.

Estimated Cost: Entrance fee is around IDR 50,000.

Location: Jl. Laksda Adisucipto No.167, Caturtunggal, Sleman Regency

Afternoon

Shop at Beringharjo Market

Dive into the bustling market atmosphere, shopping for souvenirs, batik, and local snacks—a sensory experience that captures the essence of Yogyakarta.

How to Get There

Located near Malioboro Street; easily accessible on foot or by becak.

Estimated Cost: Free to enter; shopping costs vary.

Location: Jl. Margo Mulyo No.16, Ngupasan, Yogyakarta City

Evening

Departure

As your journey concludes, take a moment to reflect on the memories made, the cultures experienced, and the adventures undertaken.

<u>How to Get There</u>

Return to Yogyakarta International Airport via taxi or ride-hailing service.

Estimated Cost: Taxi fares range from IDR 150,000 to IDR 200,000.

Location: Yogyakarta International Airport, Kulon Progo Regency

7-Day Deep Dive into Java

If you've got seven days and a little curiosity, Java will show you everything — ancient sunrise temples, underground caverns lit by heavenly beams, volcanoes that rumble beneath your feet, and people who smile like they've known you forever.

This isn't your average checklist trip. It's a full-bodied, soul-filling dive into Java's spirit.

Day 1 (Arrive in Yogyakarta — The Warm Heart of Java)

Welcome to Yogyakarta, or "Jogja" as locals call it — the island's cultural heartbeat. It's the kind of city where traditional batik artists live next to modern muralists, and street food tastes like someone's grandma made it just for you.

<u>Getting in</u>

Fly into Yogyakarta International Airport (YIA). From there, take a DAMRI bus (IDR 70K) or a Grab/taxi (IDR 150K–200K) to your hotel in Prawirotaman, a laid-back neighborhood full of cozy cafés and charm.

Unmissable Tonight
- Walk down Malioboro Street — a heady mix of smells, sounds, souvenirs, and surprises.
- Nibble on street snacks like bakpia (sweet bean pastries) or pecel lele (crispy catfish).
- Stay at Greenhost Boutique Hotel — artsy, green, and full of soul.

Tip: Carry small cash. Most stalls and vendors don't take cards.

Day 2 (Temples that Touch the Sky)

Ready to time-travel? Today's about discovering Java's ancient spirituality — from one of the world's largest Buddhist temples at sunrise, to Hindu shrines glowing at sunset.

Sunrise at Borobudur Temple

Waking up at 3:30 AM isn't easy, but trust us — seeing the mist rise over 72 stupas with Mount Merapi in the distance? Pure magic.

Location: Magelang (\~1.5 hrs from Yogya)

Getting there: Join a tour (IDR 700K–800K), or hire a private driver (IDR 450K–500K)

Entrance: IDR 500K for foreigners

Don't miss: A cup of kopi tubruk and banana fritters at a local warung afterward.

Sunset at Prambanan Temple

Later, visit Prambanan, Java's majestic Hindu temple complex. As the sun sets behind the stone towers, it feels like time stands still.

Location: East Yogya (\~30–40 min by car)

Getting there: Grab or taxi (IDR 80K–120K)

Entrance: IDR 375K

Evening extra: Watch the Ramayana Ballet under the stars — surreal and unforgettable.

(Tickets: IDR 150K–500K)

Day 3 (Nature's Calm — From Jungle Peaks to Gentle Waterfalls)

Let's slow things down and let nature lead the way.

Early Morning

Mangunan Viewpoint

Overlook rolling green hills and clouds swirling beneath you. Locals call this the "Land Above the Sky."

Location: Bantul (\~45 mins from city)

Transport: Scooter rental (IDR 70K/day) or driver (IDR 400K–500K)

Entrance: IDR 10K

Afternoon

Sri Gethuk Waterfall

A bamboo raft ride on a quiet river leads to this multi-tiered waterfall place in the trees.

Location: Gunungkidul

Entrance: IDR 20K

Raft fee: IDR 10K

Getting there

Same driver or scooter ride (1–1.5 hrs from Mangunan)

Lunch Tip

Grab nasi ayam kampung and sambal at a roadside warung — spicy, simple, and made with love.

Day 4 (Art, Coffee & Culture in Local Hands)

Today's all about slowing down and doing, not just seeing.

Try Batik Painting in Kotagede

This isn't a museum visit — it's hands-on fun. Learn how to make batik using wax and dye. Yours might be messy, but it'll be yours.

Location: Kotagede, South Yogya

Cost: IDR 100K–150K (includes your art)

Getting there: GoJek or Grab (IDR 20K–30K)

Sip Coffee in Kaliurang Highlands

Head to the hills and taste local chocolate and coffee on a peaceful plantation. The cool breeze is a bonus.

Location: Kaliurang (\~1 hour drive)

Tour cost: IDR 50K–75K

Don't miss: Ullen Sentalu Museum — it's like walking through a Javanese poem (Entry: IDR 50K)

Back in Yogya, wind down with dinner at The House of Raminten — quirky, theatrical, and deliciously local.

Day 5 (Caves, Cliffs & the Call of the Ocean)

Morning

Jomblang Cave

You're lowered down by rope into a lush, vertical cave, then guided toward the "Heaven Light" — an otherworldly beam of sunlight slicing through the darkness.

Location: Gunungkidul

Cost: IDR 500K (includes gear, lunch, and guide)

Getting there: Hire a driver (IDR 500K–600K for full day)

Afternoon

Indrayanti Beach & Timang Gondola Ride

After the cave, head to Java's rugged southern coast. Have fresh seafood by the sea, or (if you're daring) take the wild ride across crashing waves on a hand-pulled gondola at Timang Beach.

Beach entry: IDR 10K

Seafood meal: From IDR 50K

Timang gondola ride: IDR 200K

Note: It's thrilling but not for the faint of heart.

Return to Yogya for one last dreamy night.

Day 6 (Slow Train to East Java)

Java's beauty isn't just in its destinations — it's also in the journey.

Hop on a scenic train to Probolinggo, the gateway to Mount Bromo. Bring snacks, charge your phone, and enjoy a rolling view of rice paddies and volcano silhouettes.

Train: Sancaka or Wijayakusuma

Departure: Yogyakarta Tugu Station

Duration: 8 hours

Cost: IDR 300K–450K

After arrival: Take a shared jeep (IDR 75K–100K) to Cemoro Lawang village near Mount Bromo

Bundle up — it gets chilly here at night!

Day 7 (Fire & Fog — The Mighty Mount Bromo)

It's 3 AM again, but this one's worth it. You'll ride a jeep across the moonlike Sea of Sand, then hike to a ridge where the sun slowly lights up one of Indonesia's most iconic views.

Sunrise tour cost: IDR 500K–650K per jeep (can be split with others)

Park entrance: IDR 220K (weekdays), IDR 320K (weekends)

Bonus: Ride a horse to the crater (IDR 100K) or hike it on foot

Head back to Probolinggo after breakfast and either return to Yogya, continue to Surabaya, or catch a ferry to Bali for the next chapter of your journey.

Custom Itineraries

(For Families, Foodies & Explorers)

Let's be honest — one-size-fits-all travel plans don't work for everyone. Some of us are chasing toddler giggles and stroller-friendly paths. Others are ready to eat until the buttons on our pants scream for mercy. And then there are those who just want to feel something raw, real, and unforgettable.

This section is for you. It's a collection of thoughtfully crafted itineraries, each designed with a different kind of traveler in mind — complete with real-world logistics, emotional moments, and a sprinkle of magic.

For Families: Fun, Fuss-Free, and Full of Smiles (3 Days)

Day 1(Monkeys & Magic in Ubud)

Sacred Monkey Forest Sanctuary

Location: Ubud, Gianyar, Bali

Price: IDR 80,000 (adults), IDR 60,000 (kids)

How to Get There: GrabCar from central Bali or a private driver (around IDR 300,000 roundtrip from Seminyak)

Your little ones will light up as cheeky macaques swing from the trees and dart between statues in this lush, enchanted forest. Just keep your snacks zipped!

Lunch Stop

Clear Café (just 5 minutes away on foot)

What to Expect: Fresh juices, fruit platters, vegan burgers — perfect for picky eaters and health-conscious parents. Around IDR 80,000 per meal.

Evening

Location: Legong Dance at Ubud Palace

Price: IDR 100,000 per person (kids often discounted)

Show starts around 7 PM

Just a short stroll from town — no need for transport!

As the sun dips low, let your family be mesmerized by dazzling costumes and hypnotic Balinese rhythms.

Day 2 (Sandy Toes & Turtle Tales)

Morning

Splash at Sanur Beach

Location: East Coast of Bali

Price: Free access, umbrella rentals \~IDR 50,000

How to get there: GrabCar or Gojek from anywhere in Denpasar (IDR 80,000–120,000)

A quiet beach perfect for toddlers to build sandcastles and parents to sip coconut water under the shade.

Afternoon

Turtle Conservation and Education Center (Serangan Island)

Entry by donation

Help rescue turtles and, if you're lucky, release baby hatchlings into the sea!

 Just 15 minutes from Sanur (Grab or scooter)

Dinner

Seafood on the sand at Jimbaran Bay

Location: Southern Bali

Cost: Expect IDR 150,000–250,000 per person

About 25–40 mins from Sanur via Grab

The sun setting over your table as kids play in the sand? Pure family vacation bliss.

Day 3 (Waterpark Wonders)

Location: Waterbom Bali (Kuta)

Cost: IDR 540,000 (adults), IDR 327,000 (kids)

10 AM to 5 PM

GrabCar from anywhere (IDR 60,000–120,000 depending on location)

Think lazy rivers, safe toddler zones, and slides wild enough to make your teenager scream (in a good way). Clean, safe, and award-winning — it's a no-brainer.

For Foodies: A Flavor-Packed 3-Day Culinary Journey

Day 1 (The Yogyakarta Taste Tour)

Breakfast: Gudeg Yu Djum

Location: Jalan Wijilan, Yogyakarta

Cost: Around IDR 30,000

Easy Grab ride from city center (\~IDR 15,000)

Sticky jackfruit stew with rice and crispy bits — a local favorite with a sweet-savory twist.

Midday

Pasar Beringharjo food crawl

Location: Along Malioboro Street

Cost: Snacks for IDR 5,000–15,000

How to get there: Walkable, or hop on a becak (bike taxi) for fun

- Tempe mendoan, bakpia pastries, coconut ice — bring an appetite and loose clothing!

Evening

Sate Klathak Pak Pong

Location: Bantul (30 mins out of town)

Cost: IDR 50,000 per person

How to get there: Hire a GrabCar (\~IDR 70,000–90,000 roundtrip)

- Juicy skewered goat satay grilled with simplicity and served with spicy broth. Foodie heaven.

Day 2 (Bandung's Best Bites)

Brunch: Two Hands Full

Location: Sukajadi, Bandung

Cost: IDR 100,000–120,000

How to get there: GrabCar or walk if nearby

Afternoon Stroll

Jalan Braga's Art Deco cafés

Location: Central Bandung

Cost: Free to wander, cake and coffee \~IDR 40,000

Walkable zone, full of character

- Old-school patisseries meet modern vibes — sip, snack, and people-watch.

Dinner

Night Market at Cibadak Street

Cost: Street eats from IDR 10,000 per dish

GrabCar from most parts of Bandung (\~IDR 20,000–40,000)

Day 3 (Flavors of Jakarta)

Breakfast: Soto Betawi Haji Husein

Location: Central Jakarta

Cost: Around IDR 30,000

GrabCar or Gojek easily accessible

Lunch

Glodok Chinatown

Location: West Jakarta

Cost: IDR 20,000–50,000

Around IDR 40,000 by Grab from central hotels

- Dumplings, herbal tea eggs, and sizzling wok noodles — a real street food safari.

Dinner

Sky-high indulgence at SKYE Bar

Location: Level 56, BCA Tower, Thamrin

Cost: Cocktails IDR 150,000+, meals IDR 250,000+

Dress code and reservation recommended

For Explorers: Epic Adventures, Hidden Corners (3 Days)

Day 1(Chasing Fire at Mount Ijen)

Location: Banyuwangi, East Java

Cost: IDR 150,000 (weekday), IDR 200,000 (weekend)

Tour + guide + gas mask: \~IDR 600,000

Trek begins around 1 AM

- Hike under the stars, see electric-blue flames flickering from sulfur vents, then watch the sunrise and paint the crater lake turquoise. It's intense — but unforgettable.

Day 2 (Waterfalls of Wonder)

Tumpak Sewu Waterfall

Location: Lumajang

Cost: IDR 20,000

3 hours from Malang (private car \~IDR 500,000 roundtrip)

Day 3 (Your Path, Your Pace)

Option A

Whitewater Rafting at Pekalen

Location: Probolinggo

Cost: IDR 500,000 (all-in tour)

Option B

Sunrise at Mount Bromo

Location: Cemoro Lawang

Jeep + entry \~IDR 400,000

3:00 AM start (worth every groggy second)

Option C

Wander Malang

Location: Kampung Warna-Warni (Color Village)

Cost: Entry \~IDR 5,000

Explore, eat, and relax before your next adventure

FOOD & DRINK SCENE

Must-Try Local Dishes

(*Gudeg, Bakpia, Sate Klathak*)

If Yogyakarta had a love language, it would be food. Rich, soulful, and packed with personality, the city's traditional dishes are not just something you eat — they're something you feel. Whether it's the comfort of Gudeg, the smoky bite of Sate Klathak, or the sweetness of a warm Bakpia fresh from the oven, you're about to discover why Jogja is just as delicious as it is unforgettable.

Gudeg (Jogja's Signature Comfort Food)

Let's start with the queen of all Yogyakarta dishes: (Gudeg).

This sweet jackfruit stew is slow-cooked until it's melt-in-your-mouth soft, blending flavors of coconut milk, palm sugar, and traditional spices. It's typically paired with rice, tender chicken in coconut gravy, a boiled egg, and a bit of spicy sambal made with crispy beef skin (sambal krecek). The balance of sweetness and spice is subtle and comforting — the culinary equivalent of a hug from grandma.

Where to Try It: Gudeg Yu Djum – an institution in Yogyakarta. Locals have been coming here for generations.

Location: Jl. Wijilan No.167, Kraton, Yogyakarta

Cost: IDR 30,000–50,000 (\$2–3.50 USD) per serving

Open: 6 AM – 9 PM

How to Get There: Just 10 minutes from Malioboro Street. Hop on a GrabBike (about IDR 10,000) or take a traditional becak ride for the full experience.

Local Tip: Ask for the "Gudeg komplit" to get the full version with egg, chicken, and sambal. You won't regret it.

Sate Klathak (Grilled Goat, the Javanese Way)

If you're into satay, you're in for a treat. But don't expect fancy sauces or peanut dips. Sate Klathak keeps it raw and real: tender goat meat seasoned simply with salt and pepper, grilled on iron skewers (not bamboo) over hot coals. That's it. The iron rods help cook the meat from the inside too, so each bite is juicy and flavorful. It's usually served with a rich curry broth on the side, and it's downright addictive.

Where to Try It: Sate Klathak Pak Pong – this place is legendary. Expect crowds (and satisfied burps).

Location: Jl. Imogiri Timur Km.10, Bantul

Cost: IDR 30,000–45,000 (\$2–3 USD) per plate

Open: 10 AM – 11 PM

How to Get There: It's about 40 minutes from the city center. Use GrabCar (IDR 40,000–50,000 one way). Or hire a motorbike if you're feeling adventurous.

Fun Fact: "Klathak" is the sizzling sound of meat hitting the hot grill. One bite and you'll understand why this dish has a cult following.

Bakpia (Sweet, Soft, and Perfect for Gifting)

Small in size, big in flavor — Bakpia is a sweet pastry filled traditionally with mung bean paste, but these days you'll find modern twists like chocolate, cheese, and even green tea. They're soft, flaky, and slightly sweet, making them perfect for snacking or bringing home as a tasty souvenir.

Where to Get It: Bakpia Pathok 25 – probably the most famous and most loved in the city.

Location: Jl. AIP II KS Tubun No.504, Pathuk, Ngampilan

Cost: IDR 35,000–55,000 (\$2.50–3.50 USD) per box

Open: 7 AM – 10 PM

How to Get There: A short walk from Malioboro or a breezy becak ride (about IDR 10,000–15,000).

Tip: Bakpia has a short shelf life (just a few days), so plan to buy it at the end of your trip — or just eat it all right away, no judgment.

These dishes are more than local favorites — they're flavors of history, family, and everyday life in Yogyakarta. Eating them is a way of understanding the city from the inside out. So, come hungry, eat slowly, and don't be shy to use your hands — just like the locals do.

Where to Eat

(Warungs, Cafes & Food Courts)

Let's be real — one of the biggest reasons people fall in love with Yogyakarta is the food. Not just the taste, but the whole experience of it. From tiny roadside warungs run by friendly aunties to cozy cafés that feel like secret hideouts, Jogja serves up flavors and memories in equal measure.

Here's where to go when hunger strikes — and you want a plate of something that hits the soul, not just the stomach.

Warungs(Where Comfort Lives on a Plate)

Warungs are the heart of local dining. They're simple, unpretentious, and ridiculously satisfying. Most don't have menus — just point at what looks good and trust your gut. Prices are humble, and portions are often generous.

Warung Handayani

Locals adore this spot for its honest, home-style Javanese food. Everything here tastes like something your Indonesian grandma might make (if you had one).

Address: Jl. Affandi No.14, Gejayan

Cost: Around IDR 15,000–30,000 (\$1–2 USD)

Hours: 8 AM to 9 PM

Getting There: GrabBike or Gojek from Malioboro takes about 15 minutes (fare: approx. IDR 12,000)

Why you'll love it: It's affordable, authentic, and full of regulars who'll nod at you like you're already part of the neighborhood.

Warung Bu Ageng

This place mixes tradition with a touch of flair. It's owned by the husband of one of Indonesia's most respected poets, and it shows in the thoughtful flavors and artsy vibe.

Address: Jl. Tirtodipuran No.13, Mantrijeron

Cost: IDR 25,000–50,000 (\$1.70–3.50 USD)

Hours: 10 AM to 10 PM

Getting There: 20 minutes from Malioboro by becak or Grab

Don't miss: The nasi campur (mixed rice plate) — a beautiful mess of flavors — and their refreshing iced ginger tea.

Cafés (For When You Want Coffee... or Wi-Fi)

Yogyakarta's cafés are more than caffeine stations — they're social spaces, creative hubs, and places to cool off from the heat. Whether you're journaling your adventures or people-watching, there's a seat (and a snack) with your name on it.

Kopi Klotok

If you're looking for breakfast with a view, this rustic café out in the rice fields is pure bliss. Locals flock here for the nostalgic vibes and slow-cooked meals.

Address: Jl. Kaliurang Km.16.7, Pakem

Cost: IDR 10,000–25,000 (\$0.70–1.80 USD)

Hours: 7 AM to 9 PM

Getting There: 45 minutes from central Jogja; rent a scooter or GrabCar (around IDR 50,000–70,000)

What to order: The fried egg with sambal and a hot cup of kopi tubruk (unfiltered Javanese coffee). Simple, nostalgic, and soul-soothing.

Lokal Resto & Café

Trendy, youthful, and full of flair. Great for fusion dishes, stylish Instagram pics, and catching up with new friends over iced lattes.

Address: Jl. Jembatan Merah No.104C, Gejayan

Cost: IDR 40,000–80,000 (\$2.50–5.50 USD)

Hours: 10 AM to 10 PM

Getting There: 20 minutes from Malioboro by Grab

Pro tip: Their nasi goreng with salted egg is addictive. Come hungry.

Food Courts (One Stop, Many Flavors)

Craving variety? Head to a food court — perfect when you and your travel buddies want different things. These spots are lively, casual, and packed with choices.

Raminten's Kitchen Food Court

This quirky 24-hour gem is a Jogja institution. Think of it as part restaurant, part cultural performance, and totally unforgettable.

Address: Jl. Faridan M. Noto No.7, Kotabaru

Cost: IDR 20,000–60,000 (\$1.30–4 USD)

Hours: Open 24 hours

Getting There: A quick 10-minute ride from Malioboro by becak or GrabBike

Try this: Goat satay, jamu (traditional herbal drinks), and their legendary banana fritters.

Prawirotaman Night Food Court

Come here after dark for sizzling woks, glowing lanterns, and the smell of grilled goodness in the air. A foodie's dream came true.

Address: Jl. Prawirotaman, Mantrijeron

Cost: IDR 10,000–50,000 (\$0.70–3.50 USD)

Hours: 5 PM – 11 PM

Getting There: Walkable from most Prawirotaman hotels. Otherwise, Grab or a quick becak. The ride works great.

Insider tip: Don't leave without trying the Martabak Manis — an indulgent, stuffed pancake that'll ruin all future desserts for you.

Wherever you choose to dine, know this: food in Yogyakarta isn't just about eating — it's about sharing. It's warm, it's humble, and it's full of little stories. Whether you're biting into something spicy at a food court or sipping ginger tea in a rice field, these meals will stay with you long after your trip ends.

Best Street Food & Night Markets

If you're someone who believes that the best meals aren't found in fancy restaurants, but at tiny stalls under string lights, beside a smoky grill, and served with a warm smile — welcome to street food heaven. In Yogyakarta, food is more than just fuel; it's an invitation to connect, explore, and fall a little deeper in love with the city.

As the sun sets, the streets of Jogja come alive. The aroma of grilled meat, bubbling stews, and sweet coconut wafts through the air. Locals gather, students laugh over late-night snacks, and visitors like you and me get swept up in the magic of it all. Here are the top places where you can eat like a local — affordably, joyfully, and memorably.

Malioboro Street

The Iconic Strip

Malioboro is more than a shopping street. By night, it becomes a culinary carnival. Street vendors pop up like magic, mats are rolled out, and the pavement becomes your dining room.

What to Eat

- Sate Ayam (chicken satay with peanut sauce) is classic, juicy, and soul-warming.
- Lumpia Basah — soft spring rolls packed with veggies and flavor.
- Gudeg rice packs — Jogja's signature sweet jackfruit stew with egg and chicken.

- Es Dawet — a chilled coconut and jelly dessert that hits just right in the heat.

Location: Jl. Malioboro, Gedongtengen
Best Time to Go: From 6 PM onward
Price Range: Around IDR 5,000–25,000 (\$0.30–\$1.70 USD) per item
How to Get There: If you're staying central, just walk! If not, grab a GrabBike or hop in a becak (pedicab) for fun.
Insider Tip: Vendors appreciate small bills. Smile, ask questions, and enjoy the chat — it's part of the experience.

Alun-Alun Kidul (South Square)

Food, Fun, and Local Vibes

At Alun-Alun Kidul, you don't just eat — you soak in the energy. Think street musicians, flashing pedal cars, kids running around, and row upon row of food vendors.

Local Favorite

- Nasi Kucing — tiny rice portions with sambal and side dishes.
- Bakso — a hearty meatball soup loved by locals of all ages.

- Wedang Ronde — warm ginger tea with chewy mochi balls. Comfort in a cup.

Location: Jl. Alun-Alun Kidul, Patehan

When to Go: 6 PM – 11 PM

Budget Needed: IDR 3,000–20,000 (\$0.20–\$1.30 USD)

Getting There: GrabBike or scooter is quickest. It's about 10–15 minutes from Malioboro.

Don't Miss: Try walking blindfolded between the two sacred banyan trees — locals say if you succeed, your wish will come true. Harder than it looks!

Pasar Kranggan Night Market

A Local's Favorite

Want to avoid the tourist crowd and eat what the locals eat? Head to Pasar Kranggan. It's a lovely night market near Tugu Monument, filled with hidden gems that won't break your budget.

Crowd Pleasers

- Bakmi Jawa — smoky Javanese noodles cooked over charcoal.
- Pecel — steamed veggies with spicy peanut sauce that tastes homemade.
- Martabak Telor — savory, crunchy pancake stuffed with spiced egg and minced meat.

Location: Jl. Kranggan, Jetis
Best Hours: 5 PM – 10 PM

Cost Range: IDR 7,000–25,000 (\$0.50–\$1.70 USD)

Getting There: Just 10 minutes north of central Jogja. Grab is easiest.

Bonus: This is a great place for souvenir snacks and local produce too.

Sekaten Night Market

A Seasonal Feast for the Senses

If your trip aligns with the Maulid celebration (usually once a year), you're in luck. Sekaten is not just a market — it's a full-blown festival with Ferris wheels, live shows, and endless food.

Festival Favorites

- Kue Cubit — bite-sized pancakes topped with chocolate or cheese.
- Rambak — crunchy, spicy fried cow skin crackers.
- Wedang Uwuh — a fragrant herbal tea that's as unique as it sounds.

Location: Alun-Alun Utara, near Masjid Gedhe Kauman

When It Happens: Usually in the Maulid month —
check with locals!

Prices: IDR 5,000–30,000 (\$0.30–\$2 USD)

Getting There: About 10–15 minutes by Grab from
the city center.

Note: This market is seasonal, but if you're around
during Sekaten, it's an experience you'll never forget.

A Few Friendly Tips Before You Dig In

- Bring tissues or wet wipes. Most stalls won't
  have them.
- Stay hydrated. It's easy to get caught up in the
  spice and heat.
- Try something new. Even if you can't
  pronounce it, give it a shot.
- Be open. Sometimes the best dish is the one
  that looks the most unfamiliar.

Street food in Yogyakarta isn't just about eating — it's
about connecting. With flavors, with people, with
stories. It's spontaneous, satisfying, and soulful — just
like the city itself.

Vegan, Vegetarian & Halal Options

Let's be honest — traveling with dietary needs can feel like a gamble sometimes. You find a charming café, only to realize their "vegetarian" dish includes a surprise meatball. Not in Yogyakarta. This city has a heart as big as its flavor, and whether you're vegan, vegetarian, or on the lookout for fully halal mealsJogja has your back — and your taste buds.

Here's where to eat well, feel good, and not break the bank.

For Vegans & Vegetarians

One of the best things about Jogja's food scene is that many traditional dishes are already plant-based. Locals have been enjoying pecel, , and tempeh goreng long before "vegan" became trendy.

Here are a few places that'll feed your belly and your soul:

Suwe Ora Jamu

Soulful, Slow Food

If you're into herbal drinks, plant-based power bowls, and quiet nooks where you can read or journal, this is your spot. They're all about reconnecting with nature — one spoonful at a time.

Where: Jl. Nogorojo No.9, Sleman

Getting there: From Malioboro, it's about 8.5 km north — around 25–30 mins by Grab or Gojek.

Ride cost: Roughly IDR 20,000–30,000 (\$1.30–\$2 USD)

What to budget for food: IDR 25,000–60,000 (\$1.70–\$4 USD)

What it feels like: Calm, earthy, with soft music and leafy corners.

Milas Vegetarian Restaurant

A Hidden Gem for Kind Eating

Ask any vegetarian traveler in Jogja, and Milas will pop up. The food is great, but it's the peaceful garden, handmade crafts, and sense of community that make it special.

Where: Jl. Prawirotaman IV No.127B

Getting there: About 4.5 km south of Malioboro — 15 mins by Grab.

Ride cost: Around IDR 15,000–20,000 (\$1–\$1.30 USD)

Food range: IDR 20,000–55,000 (\$1.30–\$3.50 USD)

Vibe check: Feels like your favorite artist friend's backyard — calm, creative, and a bit magical.

ViaVia Jogja

Where Food Meets Soul

This isn't just a café. It's an experience. You'll meet travelers swapping stories over tempeh burgers and smoothie bowls, and maybe even sign up for a local cooking class upstairs.

Where: Jl. Prawirotaman No.30
Getting there: A quick 15-min ride from Malioboro if you're not already in the area.
Ride cost: IDR 15,000–20,000 (\$1–\$1.30 USD)
Meals start at: IDR 30,000–75,000 (\$2–\$5 USD)
Vibe: Boho-chic, always buzzing, full of stories and smiling strangers.

Halal Options

Good news — most local food in Yogyakarta is already halal. Still, if you're looking for 100% halal-certified places with great reputation and flavor, we've got you covered.

Sate Ratu

A Local Legend

The satay here is next level. The spicy red chicken satay (sate merah) is a must-try, and the owner? Possibly the nicest guy in the city — he treats every guest like royalty.

Where: Jl. Sidomukti No. 36, Sleman

Getting there: About 10 km north of Malioboro — 30–35 mins by Grab

Ride cost: IDR 25,000–35,000 (\$1.70–\$2.30 USD)

Meal cost: IDR 30,000–60,000 (\$2–\$4 USD)

Atmosphere: Friendly, clean, and full of love (and juicy skewers).

Bale Ayu Resto

Big Meals, Big Tables

This one's for families and groups. You'll find crispy fried fish, grilled chicken, and tall glasses of fresh fruit juice. All halal, all delicious.

Where: Multiple locations; try Jl. Palagan Tentara Pelajar

Getting there: Around 25 minutes by Grab from central Jogja

Ride cost: IDR 20,000–30,000 (\$1.30–\$2 USD)

Food range: IDR 25,000–70,000 (\$1.70–\$4.70 USD)

Vibe: Breezy, casual, perfect for noisy kids or big laughs.

Sop Buntut Bu Ugi

Rainy Day Comfort Food

Craving something hearty? This oxtail soup (sop buntut) will hit the spot. Rich broth, fall-off-the-bone meat, and rice to soak it all up. Heaven.

Where: Jl. Wates No.6, Bantul

Getting there: 30–35 mins southwest of the city center

Ride cost: IDR 25,000–40,000 (\$1.70–\$2.70 USD)

Food cost: Around IDR 45,000 (\$3 USD)

Vibe: Local, comforting, a hug in a bowl.

Final Foodie Tip

Yogyakarta's neighborhoods are compact enough that you can group visits by area. Planning a Prawirotaman afternoon? Try Milas for lunch, ViaVia for coffee, and wrap up with a herbal drink at Suwe Ora Jamu. Most Grab or Gojek rides in town cost less than your coffee back home.

Coffee Shops, Tea Houses & Local Drinks

Sometimes, it's not about chasing another temple or market — it's about finding a quiet corner, a cup of something warm (or ice-cold and sweet), and a little time to just breathe. Yogyakarta is a haven for these moments. The city is filled with cafés that brew local beans with pride, tea houses that feel like sanctuaries, and traditional drinks served with stories in every sip.

Whether you're a caffeine junkie, a tea traditionalist, or just someone looking for a place to slow down, here's where to go, how to get there, and what to expect — all with a local touch.

Kopi Klotok

Coffee, Culture & Rice Field Views

This is not your average café. Kopi Klotok feels more like visiting a Javanese family home than a business. There's no air-conditioning or flashy menu here — just the smell of woodfire, authentic kopi tubruk, and views of green fields stretching endlessly into the horizon. Oh, and the fried tempeh? Crispy perfection.

Location: Jl. Kaliurang KM 16.7, Pakem, Sleman

How to get there: About 45 minutes from Malioboro by Grab/Gojek (around IDR 35,000–45,000 / \$2.30–\$3 USD)

What it costs: Coffee is around IDR 6,000 (\$0.40 USD); traditional dishes start at IDR 15,000 (\$1 USD)

Vibe: Warm, nostalgic, like visiting your grandma in the countryside

Tip: Sit outside for the view — it's a sunrise lover's dream.

No.27 Coffee

Chic, Trendy & Instagram-Ready

Right in the heart of the city, No.27 is the spot if you're looking for stylish vibes, young creatives typing away on laptops, and beautifully plated drinks. It's easy to walk here from Malioboro, and their lattes come with coffee art almost too pretty to sip.

Location: Jl. Mangkubumi No.27

How to get there: 5-minute walk from Tugu Station or IDR 10,000 ride by GrabBike

What it costs: Lattes and cappuccinos from IDR 25,000 (\$1.60 USD)

Vibe: Modern, artsy, with Wi-Fi and great playlists

Must-try: Their iced salted caramel latte — sweet, bold, and unforgettable.

Lokal Coffee & Eatery

Cozy with Creative Energy

Lokal is a little quieter than the big-name spots, which makes it perfect for journaling, reading, or having deep convos over a cold brew.

Location: Jl. Jembatan Merah No.104C, Sleman

How to get there: 25-minute ride from downtown; IDR 20,000–25,000 via Grab

What it costs: Coffee and snacks range from IDR 20,000–50,000 (\$1.30–\$3.20 USD)

Vibe: Hip, hidden, and totally relaxing

Bonus: They sometimes host live acoustic sessions. Pure Jogja magic.

Taman Sari Tea House

Sip in Serenity

A short stroll from the Taman Sari Water Castle, this tiny tea house feels like a secret garden. Here, you can try wedang uwuh — a warm herbal tea made with spices like clove, ginger, and cinnamon — or sip rare Javanese flower teas in total peace.

Location: Near Taman Sari, Kraton area

How to get there: 10-minute Grab ride from Malioboro (IDR 10,000–15,000 / \$0.70–\$1 USD)

What it costs: Tea pots from IDR 15,000–35,000 (\$1–\$2.30 USD)

Vibe: Quiet, serene, with a whiff of old Jogja elegance

Try this: Jasmine tea with palm sugar — sweet, floral, and soul-soothing.

Legend Coffee

Where Games Meet Lattes

If you're traveling with friends — or just love a bit of fun with your flat white — Legend Coffee is the place to be. Open until late, filled with board games, giant Jenga, and even console setups, it's where the night turns into laughter and lattes.

Location: Jl. Abu Bakar Ali No.24, near Malioboro

How to get there: Walkable from the city center

What it costs: Coffee starts at IDR 18,000 (\$1.20 USD)

Vibe: Lively, casual, and perfect for night owls

Come at night: The crowd grows, and the energy feels like a cozy game night with strangers.

Local Drinks You've Got to Try

- Wedang Uwuh – A spicy, fiery drink with real bark and herbs. Find it near Kotagede or in traditional warungs.

Price: Around IDR 10,000 (\$0.70 USD)

Best for: Cold evenings or calming your stomach

- Es Dawet – Sweet, cold, coconut-based dessert drink with green rice flour jelly and palm sugar syrup. Perfect street snack!

Where: Along Malioboro or at Alun-Alun Selatan

Price: Around IDR 7,000–10,000 (\$0.50–\$0.70 USD)

- Teh Poci – Traditional tea served in clay teapots with chunks of rock sugar. The flavor deepens as it brews — slow sipping encouraged.

Where: Small warungs or tea stalls

Price: Around IDR 7,000–12,000 (\$0.50–\$0.80 USD)

Yogyakarta's café and tea culture isn't just about getting your caffeine fix — it's about slowing down, connecting with people, and letting the city's rhythm seep in through a simple drink. So whether you're sipping kopi klotok under the trees or trying a quirky new latte, remember: you're not just drinking — you're experiencing.

TlRAVEL STYLES & EXPERIENCES

Traveling Solo in Yogyakarta

Traveling solo isn't just about going somewhere alone — it's about discovering what moves you. And in Yogyakarta, you'll find a city that gently welcomes you in. With every smile from a street vendor, every motorbike whizzing past, and every golden temple sunrise, this city reminds you that you're never really alone.

Whether you're here to lose yourself in centuries-old ruins, dive deep into culture, or simply enjoy some "me time," Yogyakarta offers a safe, soulful experience that solo travelers often fall in love with.

Where to Stay (Without Breaking the Bank)

For solo travelers, it's important to stay somewhere safe, social, and central. Two of the best areas are **(Prawirotaman)** Yogyakarta's laid-back, artsy zone — and **(Malioboro)**, where the action never seems to stop.

Edu Hostel

Think rooftop pool, friendly faces, and a fun common area to meet fellow travelers.

Location: Jl. Letjen Suprapto No.17

Cost: Dorm beds from IDR 120,000 (\~\$8 USD)

The Capsule Malioboro

A little more privacy with your own pod-style bed, but still social enough to mingle.

Location: Near Malioboro Street

Cost: IDR 150,000 (\~\$10 USD)

Both spots are close to cafes, cultural spots, and street food — basically, your solo adventure basecamps.

Chill Spots for Solo Vibes

ViaVia Café (Prawirotaman)

This place has it all: travel info, live music, delicious food, and a chance to join local tours or cooking classes. Sit outside, order a smoothie bowl, and just watch the world pass by.

Meals start at IDR 40,000 (\~\$3 USD)

Ride from city center via Grab: \~IDR 10,000–20,000

Hutan Kota Baciro (City Forest)

If you're craving peace and shade, grab your book and head here. Locals come for picnics or quiet walks.

Location: Baciro, just east of the train station

Entry: Free

Grab or Gojek: IDR 12,000–15,000

Experiences Perfect for Going Solo

Sunrise at Borobudur Temple

Trust me, this is one of those "you had to be there" moments. Join a small group tour, watch the sun paint the sky, and connect with other travelers over coffee and awe.

Location: Magelang, about 1.5 hours from Yogya

Cost: IDR 650,000 (\~\$42 USD) including transport

Book tours via your hostel, Klook, or GetYourGuide

Street Food Stroll on Malioboro Street

This is where Yogyakarta truly comes alive at night. Try bakpia, fried banana, or sate on the go, and strike up conversations with curious locals.

Budget: IDR 50,000 (\~\$3.25 USD) will get you a mini feast!

Creative Workshops (Batik & Silver Making)

A great way to meet people and make something beautiful with your own hands.

Locations

Winotosastro Batik House (Jl. Tirtodipuran)

Kota Gede Silver Workshops

Classes range from IDR 150,000–250,000

Duration: Around 2 hours

A Quick Word on Safety

Yogyakarta is one of Indonesia's safest cities, and locals are genuinely kind — often going out of their way to help. Still, keep these tips in mind:

- Stick to ride-hailing apps like Grab or Gojek instead of random taxis.
- Avoid dim alleys late at night, especially outside central areas.
- Always carry a digital copy of your passport, and don't flaunt valuables.

Tip

Here's the thing about solo travel in Yogyakarta: you arrive with a little nervous excitement, and before you know it, the city starts feeling like an old friend. You'll meet strangers who share your table, locals who teach you how to say "terima kasih" with a smile, and you'll walk away with stories no one else could write for you.

So go ahead — take that solo trip. Yogyakarta is ready for you.

Couples' Getaways & Romantic Spots

Yogyakarta has a way of wrapping around your heart. It's not just the ancient temples or the scenic hills—it's the way the city slows you down, makes you notice the breeze, the colors in the sky, and the quiet smiles you share with someone special. If you're traveling with your partner, this city is the perfect backdrop for connection, romance, and a little magic.

Here's how to make it unforgettable—for both of you.

Where to Stay

Cozy Nooks and Romantic Retreats

Let's be honest—when you're on a couple's getaway, where you sleep really matters. Whether you're into quiet garden views, starlit dinners, or private pools, these places will make your time together feel special.

Dusun Jogja Village Inn

Think candlelit gardens, traditional Javanese design, and an atmosphere so peaceful you'll feel like time has stopped. It's charming, quiet, and intimate.

Location: Prawirotaman

Cost: From IDR 850,000 (\~\$55 USD) per night

About 15 minutes from the airport by Grab (IDR 50,000–70,000)

Hyatt Regency Yogyakarta

Fancy something more luxurious? This place has manicured lawns, a beautiful golf course, and even romantic horse-drawn carriage rides. You'll feel pampered every second.

Location: Jalan Palagan Tentara Pelajar

Cost: From IDR 1.3 million (\~\$85 USD) per night

Around 30 minutes from the city center (Grab IDR 60,000)

Villa Rosseno

This one's a hidden gem. Private villas, your own pool, and sunsets over the rice fields. It's peaceful, personal, and perfect for couples who want to feel like they're in their own little world.

Location: Kasihan, Bantul

Cost: From IDR 1.5 million (\~\$100 USD) per night

Roughly 25 minutes by Grab (IDR 40,000–50,000)

Romantic Experiences That Feel Like a Movie

Sunset at Ratu Boko Palace

If you only do one romantic thing in Yogyakarta, make it this. The ancient palace ruins are stunning, but when the sun dips behind the horizon? It's pure magic.

Location: About 30 minutes east of the city

Cost: IDR 140,000 (\~\$9 USD)

Grab or scooter rental (\~IDR 50,000–60,000)

Candlelit Dinner at Abhayagiri

The setting: a terrace overlooking the majestic Prambanan Temple and distant Mount Merapi. Add soft lighting, amazing food, and that "just us" feeling.

Location: Sumberwatu Heritage Resort

Cost: Around IDR 100,000–250,000 per person

30–40 minutes from downtown by Grab

Wander Taman Sari Water Castle

Early mornings here feel like stepping into a fairytale. Quiet pools, secret passages, and old-world romance make it perfect for couples—especially if you love taking dreamy photos together.

Location: Near the Kraton (Sultan's Palace)

Entry: IDR 15,000 (\~\$1 USD)

Easily walkable from central hotels or take a short Grab ride

Private Batik or Pottery Class

Want to create something together? These workshops are fun, hands-on, and surprisingly romantic. Plus, you get to keep your masterpiece!

Location: Found in Prawirotaman or Kota Gede

Cost: Around IDR 200,000–350,000 per couple

Classes run about 1.5 to 2 hours

Love After Dark (Nighttime Magic)

Alun-Alun Kidul (Southern Square)

It's quirky, it's fun, and it's a local tradition. Try walking between the twin banyan trees blindfolded—it's said that if you succeed, your love is true! Stick around to ride those glowing, pedal-powered "bubble cars."

Location: South of the Sultan's Palace

Cost: Free (bikes rent for IDR 20,000)

Walkable from many hotels or a quick Grab away

Stargazing at Bukit Bintang

Want something simple and meaningful? Head to this lookout point, grab some roasted corn from a roadside stall, and watch the stars come out. Some of the best conversations happen under skies like this.

Location: Along the road to Gunung Kidul

Cost: Free

About 45 minutes by Grab (\~IDR 80,000–100,000)

Practical information

Sometimes, the best trips aren't about ticking off a list—they're about slowing down, being present, and sharing small moments. That's exactly what Yogyakarta offers couples. A stolen kiss on a quiet street. A deep talk over kopi tubruk. A surprise view that takes your breath away.

So go ahead—wander slowly, laugh loudly, and fall in love with each other all over again, right here in Yogya.

Yogyakarta for Families with Kids

Traveling with kids? Don't worry—Yogyakarta isn't just for temple-hopping culture lovers. It's a city full of play, wonder, and those "wow" moments that make traveling as a family so worth it. Whether your little ones love animals, art, or just running wild in nature, Yogya wraps it all up in one beautiful, easy-to-explore package.

So here's a friendly guide to places your kids will genuinely enjoy—and ones you'll love too.

Where Learning Feels Like Play

Taman Pintar Science Park

Let your kids be curious—here, they'll get their hands on everything from water experiments to dinosaur models and mini science shows. There's even a planetarium if they're into stars and space.

Location: Jl. Panembahan Senopati No.1A (near Malioboro)

Cost: About IDR 20,000–25,000 (around \$1.30 USD)

From Malioboro, you can walk (10–15 mins) or take a Grab for IDR 15,000–20,000.

- Parents, grab a cold drink while they play—there's a small café too.

Gembira Loka Zoo

This is more than just a zoo—it's a peaceful green space where kids can meet elephants, feed deer, and even ride a little train. It's stroller-friendly and great for winding down on a slower day.

Location: Jl. Kebun Raya No.2, Kotagede

Cost: IDR 60,000 adults, IDR 45,000 kids

Takes 20–25 minutes by Grab, around IDR 25,000–35,000 from the city center.

Tip: Go early—it gets warm by noon.

Sindu Kusuma Edupark

Mini amusement park vibes with big family energy—giant Ferris wheel, bumper cars, and arcade fun. It's a bit cheesy in the best way, and great for late afternoons.

Location: Jl. Jambon, Sleman

Cost: Entry from IDR 25,000; rides from IDR 10,000–35,000

About 25 mins by Grab from Malioboro or Prawirotaman (IDR 30,000–40,000)

Creative Little Hands Welcome

Kids' Batik Painting Workshop

Let them wear an apron and get messy with wax, brushes, and dyes as they create their very own batik artwork. A perfect mix of tradition and play.

Location: Rumah Batik Winotosastro, Prawirotaman

Cost: Around IDR 100,000–150,000 per child

Walkable in Prawirotaman. From Malioboro: Grab for IDR 20,000.

- The staff are incredibly patient with kids—it's a hit for ages 5 and up.

Silver Jewelry Making (for Tweens & Teens)

Let your older ones create something shiny they'll actually keep. These workshops guide them in crafting simple rings or pendants—real silver, real pride.

Location: Studios in Kota Gede, like HS Silver or Studio 76

Cost: From IDR 250,000–300,000

Around 30 mins by Grab (IDR 30,000–40,000).

- Best part? You'll both come out feeling like artists.

Nature Moments That Calm and Inspire

Taman Sari (Water Castle)

It's like stepping into a storybook—ancient pools, secret staircases, and underground passages. Your kids will feel like they're on a treasure hunt.

Location: Near Kraton Yogyakarta

Cost: IDR 15,000 per person

About a 15–20 minute walk from Malioboro, or Grab for IDR 15,000.

- Great for early mornings or late afternoons when it's cooler.

Kalibiru National Park

A peaceful forest park with zip lines and photo spots perched high above the trees. If your kids love a little adventure, this is worth the trip.

Location: Menoreh Hills, Kulon Progo

Cost: Entry IDR 10,000–20,000; zipline IDR 30,000–50,000

About 1.5 hours away—rent a driver (IDR 500,000/day) or join a family tour.

- Pack snacks and enjoy the views—you'll feel refreshed by the silence.

Parangtritis Beach

This is where sunsets meet sandcastles. You'll find ponies to ride, ATVs to rent, and miles of open beach to just... run wild.

Location: About 45 km south of the city

Free entry; IDR 5,000 for parking; pony rides IDR 30,000–50,000

Grab car from city: around IDR 60,000–70,000 (45 minutes)

- It's windy, wild, and wonderful—bring a kite if you have one!

Eating Out With Kids (Without Tears)

Warung Heru

Casual, cheerful, and tasty. Local dishes with just enough options to please fussy eaters.

Location: Jl. Prawirotaman

Cost: IDR 25,000–60,000 per meal

Walkable if staying nearby, Grab from Malioboro: IDR 20,000

- Try the fried chicken—it's crispy and comforting.

Milas Vegetarian Café

There's a reading corner, a little pond, a garden, and enough healthy food choices to feel like you're doing parenting right.

Location: Jl. Prawirotaman IV

Meals: IDR 30,000–75,000

Walkable in the Prawirotaman area, Grab from elsewhere: IDR 20,000–25,000

- It's peaceful and feels like a secret garden.

House of Raminten

A feast for the senses—colorful décor, unusual dishes, and a vibe that'll keep kids engaged while you enjoy your meal.

Location: Jl. FM Noto

Meals: IDR 25,000–50,000

15-minute Grab ride from most central hotels (IDR 20,000–25,000)

- The menu is quirky, and the portions are perfect for sharing.

<u>Practical information</u>

Yogyakarta has this gentle energy that makes traveling with kids feel less chaotic. People here love families—you'll notice the smiles, the extra chairs, the unexpected kindness from strangers. So don't stress too much about schedules. Let your days unfold. Let your kids be curious. And don't forget to take moments to just enjoy this new world together.

Because in the end, it's not just about where you go—it's about who you explore it with.

Backpacking Routes & Hostels

Yogyakarta is one of those magical places where you can live large even on a small budget. It's the kind of city that gives you history, street food, art, temples, beach sunsets, and hostel hangouts all in one go. For backpackers? It's paradise.

Here's a guide made just for you—whether you've got 3 days or a full week, whether you're chasing temples or cheap eats, this one's for those who travel with open hearts and light backpacks.

Sample Backpacking Route (3–7 Days)

Day 1–2: Dive Into the City

Start off in Malioboro or Prawirotaman—both are great bases with hostels, cafes, and things to see. Wander the alleys of Kraton (the Sultan's Palace), get lost in the water palace of Taman Sari, and haggle for batik in the markets.

Entry fees: IDR 10,000–20,000 per site (\~\$0.60–\$1.30 USD).

You can walk or take a Grab Bike (IDR 10,000–15,000 per ride).

Day 3–4: Temple Days

Book a day trip to Borobudur for sunrise—yes, it's early, but trust me, the view is worth it. Combine it with Prambanan and the ruins at Ratu Boko if you've got the energy.

Borobudur: IDR 75,000–100,000 (regular); sunrise tour around IDR 250,000–300,000.

Rent a scooter for IDR 60,000/day or join a group tour (IDR 150,000–200,000).

Day 5–6: Nature Calls

Adventure time! Head to Goa Jomblang—a vertical cave with a dramatic light beam. Or go tubing through Pindul Cave for a splash of fun.

Goa Jomblang: IDR 450,000–500,000 (includes gear, guide, and lunch).

Shared vans from Yogyakarta start from IDR 150,000 round trip.

Day 7: Chill Beach Day

After all that exploring, reward yourself with a chill day at Parangtritis Beach or head to Wediombo for fewer crowds. Bring a towel, order a coconut, and let the sea breeze do the rest.

Entry: IDR 5,000–10,000; Grab or scooter rental costs around IDR 60,000.

Where to Crash (Hostels We Love)

Hostels in Yogyakarta aren't just cheap—they've got personality. Whether you're the social butterfly or the introverted explorer, there's a spot for you.

The Capsule Malioboro

A pod-style hostel right in the heart of downtown. You get privacy, free breakfast, and instant access to shops and street food.

Location: Jl. Sosrowijayan (2 min from Malioboro Street)

Cost: IDR 100,000/night (\~\$6.50 USD)

Best for: First-time Yogya visitors who want convenience.

Good Karma Hostel

Chilled-out vibes, hammock garden, communal dinners, and lovely staff who'll feel like your temporary family.

Location: Prawirotaman area (great café scene nearby)

Cost: IDR 90,000–100,000

Best for: Meeting fellow travelers and slowing down.

Sae Sae Hostel

Homey and full of charm. This one's a little off the main track, but that's what makes it special. Also, there are cats.

Location: Caturtunggal, Sleman

Cost: IDR 90,000–120,000

Best for: Peaceful stays, creatives.

OstiC House

Welcoming staff, cozy bunks, and nightly movie screenings. If you're tired of being "on" all the time, this is your chill zone.

Location: Suryodiningratan area

Cost: IDR 100,000–130,000

Best for: Laid-back explorers and Netflix fans.

Backpacking Tips

Rent a scooter: Just IDR 60,000 a day and you'll feel the freedom immediately. Don't forget your helmet (and confidence).

Eat local: Street food like gudeg or bakmi will fill your belly for under IDR 20,000.

Bring a reusable bottle: Most hostels have water refill stations. Stay hydrated and skip the plastic.

Get a local SIM: Telkomsel works well—10–15 GB for around IDR 50,000. Totally worth it.

Take your time: You don't need to "see it all." Yogyakarta is about the feeling, not just the checklist.

Cultural involvement

Workshops, Classes & Home Stays

Some places are meant to be seen. Others—like Yogyakarta—are meant to be felt. There's something special about this city that pulls you in softly and makes you feel like you belong. And the best way to experience that magic? Don't just visit—participate.

Here are a few meaningful ways you can go beyond the postcards and connect with the real soul of Yogya.

Make Your Own Batik

A Colorful Piece of You

Batik isn't just a souvenir—it's a story written in wax and dye. Instead of buying one off a rack, why not create your own? In a batik workshop, you'll sit beside local artists, trace patterns with molten wax, and dip your creation into vivid dyes. It's surprisingly relaxing—and more rewarding than you might think.

Location: Batik Winotosastro, Jl. Tirtodipuran (near Prawirotaman area)

Open daily, 9 AM–4 PM

Cost: Around IDR 100,000–150,000 (includes materials and guidance)

Grab ride from Malioboro: approx. 15 minutes, IDR 15,000

- You'll leave with a cloth that holds more than color—it holds a memory.

Join a Home-Style Cooking Class

If you've fallen in love with Gudeg, Tempe Mendoan, or Javanese sambal, it's time to learn the secrets behind them. Cooking classes here aren't just about food—they're about storytelling, spice sniffing, and belly laughs shared over a hot stove.

Location: ViaVia Jogja, Jl. Prawirotaman

Most classes start at 9 AM and run 3–4 hours

Cost: IDR 250,000–350,000 (includes market tour, ingredients, and feast!)

Walking distance if you're staying in the hip Prawirotaman area

Bonus: Vegan, vegetarian, and gluten-free options are often available—you just have to ask.

Play a Gamelan or Learn Traditional Dance

Ever felt the deep, calming rhythm of a Javanese gamelan orchestra? You don't have to be a musician to enjoy this. You'll learn to strike gongs, bars, and drums in a way that feels more meditative than musical. Some classes also offer beginner's Javanese dance sessions—and they're just as enchanting.

Location: Yogyakarta Cultural Center, Jl. Panembahan Senopati

Afternoon sessions, usually 2 PM–4 PM

Cost: IDR 75,000–100,000 per session

About 10 minutes from Malioboro by Grab or becak (IDR 20,000–25,000)

- You may not be stage-ready after one class—but your heart will definitely be fuller.

Stay with a Local Family

Sleep, Eat, and Live the Javanese Way

If you're the kind of traveler who seeks connection more than comfort, a homestay is for you. Sharing meals, swapping stories, hearing roosters in the morning—it's all part of the charm. Many hosts even offer to show you around their neighborhoods, take you to local markets, or teach you how to make Javanese coffee the right way.

Top picks

Location: Ndalem Suratin Homestay (close to the Kraton area)

Around IDR 120,000–200,000/night (often includes breakfast)

Location: Omah Kotagede Homestay (located in Yogyakarta's silver craft district)

Around IDR 150,000–250,000/night

- If you're lucky, you might be invited to a family event or ceremony. And trust us—those are the stories you'll carry home.

Learn the Language

Even Just a Little

Even knowing a handful of words in Bahasa Indonesia can open doors. Try "Apa kabar?" (How are you?) or "Enak sekali!" (So delicious!). Locals will light up when they hear you make the effort, no matter how small.

Location: Wisma Bahasa, Sleman

Cost: IDR 100,000–200,000 for a one-hour crash course

- You can also find free mini-lessons in some hostels or even chat with your homestay host over a cup of tea.

Practical information

You Don't Have to Be a Spectator

In Yogyakarta, you're not just a visitor—you're a welcomed guest. The people here aren't trying to impress you with skyscrapers or speed. They want to share their art, their food, their stories—and if you're open to it, their hearts. Whether you're holding a wax-dipped canting pen, stirring sambal in a warm kitchen, or tapping along to a gamelan beat, you're not watching from the outside anymore.

You're a part of the rhythm. And that rhythm stays with you.

DAY TRIPS & ADVENTURES BEYOND

Parangtritis Beach & Sandboarding

There's something about the sound of crashing waves and the feel of salty wind in your hair that makes you forget the world for a moment. That's exactly what happens when you arrive at Parangtritis Beach — a place where nature shows off and the stories of ancient Javanese spirits hang thick in the air.

Just about an hour's ride from the heart of Yogyakarta, Parangtritis is where locals go when they need to breathe deeper, play harder, or just watch the sun melt into the Indian Ocean. It's wild, a little mysterious, and bursting with adventure.

How to get there

You've got a few options, depending on how you like to travel:

Rent a scooter (IDR 80,000–100,000 per day) and ride down yourself — the drive is scenic, filled with rolling fields and glimpses of village life.

Hire a private driver (around IDR 500,000 for a full day) if you'd rather kick back and let someone else handle the roads.

Public transport? It's possible! Hop on a TransJogja bus to Terminal Giwangan, then switch to a local minibus (colt) heading to Parangtritis. The whole trip costs around IDR 25,000–30,000 and takes a bit longer — but it's part of the adventure.

Location: Parangtritis, Bantul Regency — about 28 km south of Yogyakarta.

Things to Do (Besides Watching the Sunset)

Sandboarding at Gumuk Pasir

Think snowboarding, but on soft dunes. It's thrilling, messy, and pure fun. You can rent a board for around IDR 100,000–150,000, which often includes a quick tutorial. Don't worry if you're a beginner — falling is half the fun.

Ride an ATV on the beach

Feel the wind in your face and the thrill of zipping along the shoreline. Rentals start from IDR 50,000 for 15 minutes.

Chill on the beach

Or do absolutely nothing except let the wind tug at your thoughts. This place is made for it.

Beach Entrance Fee: IDR 10,000 per person

Best Time to Visit

Come in the late afternoon. That's when the beach is bathed in golden light, the heat eases, and the sunset — oh, the sunset — it's the kind that leaves you speechless. Just one thing: the water here can be rough, so swimming is not advised.

What to Eat Nearby

You won't go hungry. There are small seaside warungs serving grilled seafood, fresh coconuts, and local snacks. Try some pisang goreng (fried bananas) or a plate of spicy sambal fish. Expect to spend around IDR 60,000–80,000 for two people.

Before you leave, take a moment to sit quietly. Locals believe this beach is sacred — tied to the legend of Ratu Kidul, the Queen of the Southern Sea. Whether you believe it or not, you'll feel something special here. Something ancient and powerful.

Cave Tubing, Forest Camping & Village Life

Let's be real — sometimes, you just want to get out of the city, shake the dust off your sandals, and feel something real. Yogyakarta may be packed with art, culture, and history, but beyond the bustle lies an untamed, nature-rich world that's calling your name. If your soul's craving caves, trees, and stories from the villages, you're in the right place.

Glide Through Darkness at Goa Pindul (Cave Tubing)

Imagine this: you're lying back on a tube, floating down a river inside a cave, staring up at rock formations older than you can imagine, while sunlight peeks through cracks above. This isn't a dream — it's Goa Pindul.

Location: Bejiharjo Village, Gunungkidul (about 1.5 hours southeast of Yogyakarta)

How to get there

Rent a scooter (IDR 80,000–100,000/day) or hire a driver (IDR 500,000–600,000/day).

Tour packages from Yogyakarta are also available and affordable — many start at IDR 150,000/person, including transportation, gear, and a guide.

Cost: Around IDR 100,000–125,000 per person for the tubing experience, which includes everything you need (helmet, life vest, guide, and sometimes even a GoPro shot if you're lucky).

Why it's worth it

The water's cool, the air smells like earth and adventure, and your guide will probably tell you some fascinating (and sometimes hilarious) stories about the cave. Some even sing to show off the cave's amazing acoustics!

Sleep Under the Stars in Mangunan Pine Forest

Need to hit pause? Head to Mangunan, where towering pine trees sway above a quiet, misty forest that feels like it's from a fairytale. It's the kind of place that makes you want to ditch your phone and roast marshmallows instead.

Location: Hutan Pinus Mangunan, Bantul Regency (around 45–60 minutes from downtown Yogyakarta)

How to get there

Scooter or private car is your best bet. Grab/Gojek can drop you off, but catching one back might be tricky, so plan accordingly.

Cost

Entrance: Just IDR 5,000–10,000.

Tent rental: IDR 150,000–250,000/night, or bring your own gear if you're feeling extra adventurous.

Why it's magical

Wake up to fog gently rolling between the trees. Catch sunrise at Bukit Panguk Kediwung, or walk hand-in-hand under lantern-lit paths at Pinus Pengger. And if you're lucky, there might be a local art performance under the stars.

Experience Real Village Life in Nglanggeran

Want to slow down and connect with something — and someone — genuine? Nglanggeran Village, located inside an ancient volcanic crater, is one of the most heartwarming spots around. It's the kind of place where kids wave as you pass by, the air smells like woodsmoke and cacao, and life runs on a rhythm that makes sense.

Location: Nglanggeran, Gunungkidul (around 1 hour east of Yogyakarta)

How to get there

Rent a scooter or car. You can also join a community-based tour for convenience and a more experience (roughly IDR 400,000–600,000/day with transport and guide).

<u>Cost</u>

Homestays: Around IDR 100,000–200,000/night, often with meals included

Activities (chocolate making, traditional cooking, farming): IDR 75,000–150,000

Hiking the ancient volcano: Free or donation-based (local guides are available for a small tip)

Why this place steals hearts

You'll hike an ancient volcano at sunrise, learn to make chocolate from scratch, and share stories over warm tea with your host family. There's no rush here — just good people, good food, and moments you'll remember long after you've left.

Final Tips from One Adventurer to Another

Be kind and curious: The locals here are incredibly generous. A warm smile and a few words in Bahasa (like terima kasih)

CULTURE, LANGUAGE & LOCAL LIFE

Yogyakarta's Role in Javanese Culture

Yogyakarta isn't just a place you visit—it's a place you feel. Carry away on the island of Java, this city doesn't just preserve tradition—it lives it, breathes it, and generously shares it with anyone who walks its streets with curiosity and respect. If Indonesia had a cultural heartbeat, it would echo from the very core of Jogja.

The Living Royal City

Where the Sultan Still Rules

What sets Yogyakarta apart from every other Indonesian city is this: it still has a king. Not just in spirit, but in title and role. The beloved Sri Sultan Hamengkubuwono X isn't just a symbolic figure—he's both the cultural leader and governor of this special region. His presence isn't carried away in dusty history books; it's felt in the pulse of daily life.

At the center of it all is the Kraton—the royal palace. But don't expect something cold or sterile. This palace is alive with soft-spoken courtiers, spiritual ceremonies, and the faint, mesmerizing sound of gamelan music drifting through the courtyards.

Where: Jl. Rotowijayan Blok No. 1, Kraton, Yogyakarta

How to Get There: From Malioboro Street, you can hop on a becak (a local pedicab) for around IDR 10,000–15,000 (roughly \$0.60–\$1) or grab a GoJek ride via app.

Cost: Entrance is IDR 15,000 (about \$1). Local guides are available—and worth every bit for the insights they offer.

Art Is Life

Batik, Shadow Puppets & the Sound of Gamelan

Culture in Yogyakarta isn't something locked away behind glass. Here, art is lived.

Batik isn't just fabric—it's storytelling on cloth. You'll see women gracefully painting hot wax patterns on cotton, each design whispering tales from generations past. For a hands-on experience, try a workshop at Batik Winotosastro or Rumah Batik Roro Djonggrang.

Expect to pay around IDR 75,000–150,000 (\~\$5–10) to create your own piece.

Wayang Kulit (Shadow Puppetry) is something magical. Picture intricate leather puppets dancing behind a backlit screen, narrating epics that stretch back hundreds of years. You can catch a performance at the Sonobudoyo Museum near the Kraton, usually for just IDR 20,000–30,000 (\~\$1.30–2). The experience? Priceless.

And then there's the gamelan—a hypnotic Javanese orchestra of gongs, metallophones, and bamboo flutes. The moment you hear it, you'll know: this is the sound of Java's spirit.

Where the Past and Future Shake Hands

Jogja is known as the City of Students, home to institutions like Gadjah Mada University and the Indonesian Institute of the Arts (ISI).

Here, tradition and modern creativity meet. A batik artist might also be a graffiti muralist. A gamelan musician might be remixing ancient melodies with modern beats.

In Jogja, culture doesn't stand still. It evolves—respectfully, beautifully.

Bahasa Indonesia Basics for Travelers

One of the most heartwarming things you'll discover in Yogyakarta is how genuinely friendly and welcoming the people are. And while many locals speak a bit of English—especially in touristy areas—learning just a few words of Bahasa Indonesia can completely change your travel experience.

Seriously, you don't need to be fluent. Just trying is enough. Locals light up when you greet them in their own language, and often, that little effort can spark warm laughter, a meaningful chat, or even a small discount at a market stall.

Super Simple Words & Phrases That Work Like Magic

Your Bahasa Indonesia Survival Kit

You don't need to be fluent to have a great time in Yogyakarta—but knowing a few local words can go a *long* way. It shows respect, builds instant connection, and—let's be honest—it might even earn you a better price at a street stall!

Here are some super handy phrases that are easy to remember and super useful in real-life situations. Feel free to bookmark this page or keep it in your pocket as your personal travel cheat sheet.

Basic Greetings & Manners

- **Hello**
  Halo — pronounced **HAH-lo**
  A simple, friendly greeting that works any time

of day.

- **Good Morning**
  Selamat pagi — pronounced **suh-LAH-maht PAH-gee**
  Use this before noon. Say it with a smile, and you'll get one back.
- **Thank You**
  Terima kasih — pronounced **tuh-REE-mah KAH-see**
  You'll use this *a lot*—locals really appreciate it.
- **You're Welcome**
  Sama-sama — pronounced **SAH-mah SAH-mah**
  A kind and casual way to respond after someone thanks you.

Everyday Essentials

- **Excuse Me / Sorry**
  Maaf — pronounced **MAH-ahf**
  Whether you're bumping into someone or asking for help, this is your go-to.
- **Yes / No**
  Iya / Tidak — pronounced **EE-yah /**

TEE-dahk

Easy and important!

- **How much is this?**

  Berapa harganya? — pronounced
  buh-RAH-pah har-GAHN-yah

  Essential for shopping, from souvenirs to snacks.

Food & Fun Phrases

- **Delicious!**

  Enak sekali! — pronounced **EH-nahk
  seh-KAH-lee**

  Say this after enjoying that heavenly gudeg or bakpia!

- **I don't understand**

  Saya tidak mengerti — pronounced **SAH-yah
  TEE-dahk meng-ER-tee**

  No worries! People will be patient if you say this kindly.

- **Can you help me?**

  Bisa bantu saya? — pronounced **BEE-sah
  BAHN-too SAH-yah?**

  Whether you're lost or confused, this will often get you a helping hand.

Practical information

You don't have to get the pronunciation perfect—your effort will go a long way. Indonesians are some of the friendliest people you'll meet, and even a few words in their language will light up their faces. Practice when you can, laugh off any mistakes, and enjoy the little moments of connection.

Insider Tip: Download the Bahasa Indonesia pack on Google Translate so you can use it offline. It helps a lot when you're exploring smaller villages or local neighborhoods where English might not be widely spoken.

Where to Practice Without Pressure

Pasar Beringharjo or Pasar Kotagede: Walk through these buzzing local markets and try your Bahasa as you shop for batik, spices, or street snacks. Locals here are kind and often amused by foreigners trying the language—expect smiles, patience, and maybe a better deal!

Warungs and food stalls: Say "Selamat malam" (good evening) when you grab dinner at a roadside stall or "Enak!" when you enjoy a meal. It's the best way to connect beyond just pointing at a menu.

Workshops and community classes: Whether it's learning batik or taking a cooking class, locals are always excited to teach you not just their craft—but a few words, too.

Why It's Totally Worth It

Trying to speak Bahasa Indonesia, even just a little, is one of the most respectful and rewarding things you can do while visiting Yogyakarta. Locals genuinely appreciate it. Even if your pronunciation is off, they'll likely cheer you on with a wide smile or correct you gently in a way that feels more like friendship than criticism.

At the end of the day, it's not about being perfect—it's about being present and open. Language, even in its simplest form, is a beautiful bridge.

Religion, Traditions & Local Festivals

Where faith isn't just practiced—it's lived, celebrated, and quietly woven into every corner of daily life.

In Yogyakarta, tradition isn't trapped in museums or old books. It's alive. You'll feel it in the rhythm of the prayer calls echoing across rooftops, in the graceful flick of a dancer's fingers, and in the colorful chaos of street parades. It's a place where spirituality, culture, and celebration blend seamlessly—and if you let it, it'll move you in the most unexpected ways.

Religion

The Heartbeat of Everyday Life

Yogyakarta is predominantly Muslim, and you'll likely hear the Adzan (call to prayer) as early as dawn. But here, faith isn't about grandeur—it's gentle, humble, and beautifully integrated into the daily flow. You'll see families praying in quiet courtyards, students pausing their routines for afternoon prayer, and community life centering around the neighborhood mosque.

Yet, this city is also quietly diverse. You'll find Christian churches, Hindu temples, and Buddhist shrines placed among homes and shops. And then there's Kejawen—a spiritual blend of animism, Hinduism, Buddhism, and Islam that's uniquely Javanese. It doesn't shout. It whispers.

Location: Masjid Gedhe Kauman (The Great Mosque)

Where: Right next to the Kraton (the royal palace)

How to Get There: A 10-minute walk or a Rp 20,000 becak ride from Malioboro

Why Go: Built in 1773, it's more than a mosque—it's a piece of living history.

Traveler Tip: Dress modestly when visiting mosques. For women, a headscarf isn't always required, but covering your arms and legs is a sign of respect. Most mosques provide sarongs and scarves at the entrance if needed.

Traditions Still Going Strong

This isn't a city that's "held onto" tradition—it's one that's proudly living it. Elders still chant Javanese prayers. Puppet masters still tell tales older than the Sultanate. And teenagers? They're still dancing to gamelan music.

Wayang Kulit (Shadow Puppetry)

Where: Sonobudoyo Museum, near Alun-Alun Utara

When: Nightly performances (usually start at 8 PM)

How to Get There: 10-minute walk from Malioboro or a cheap Grab ride (\~Rp 15,000)

Entry: Rp 20,000 (\~\$1.30 USD)

Why You'll Love It: These aren't just puppet shows—they're centuries-old legends told in shadows, with live gamelan music and incense in the air. Bring patience and curiosity—it's slow, poetic, and powerful.

Royal Dance Performances at the Kraton

Where: Inside the palace compound

Entry: Rp 15,000 (includes palace tour)

How to Get There: Easily walkable or take a pedicab

What to Expect: Costumed dancers glide across the floor, each movement telling a story. You don't need to speak Javanese to feel it.

Everyday Art Meets Ancient Wisdom

Tradition here isn't just for performance—it's something people do. From hand-making batik to crafting silver jewelry, the locals still honor time-worn skills passed down through generations.

Location: Batik Workshop (Tirtodipuran or KotaGede)

How to Get There: GoJek or Grab from Malioboro (Rp 20,000–30,000)

Cost: Rp 100,000–150,000 to make your own batik

Why Try It: There's something incredibly calming about slowly painting wax onto cloth, surrounded by stories and warm smiles. You'll leave with a piece of art—and a little more appreciation for the patience it takes to create it.

Festivals

When the City Feels Like One Big Celebration

If you ever want to see Yogyakarta's spirit in full bloom, come during a festival. These aren't just events—they're deeply rooted, wildly joyful explosions of faith, community, and tradition.

Sekaten Festival

When: Around the Prophet Muhammad's birthday (dates vary by Islamic calendar)

Where: Around the Kraton and Alun-Alun Utara

What It's Like: Gamelan orchestras, food stalls, ferris wheels, and a sacred royal procession that feels straight out of another era. It's loud, colorful, and unforgettable.

Cost: Free

How to Get There: Walk from Malioboro or take a becak for Rp 20,000–25,000

Labuhan Ceremony

Where: Either Mount Merapi or Parangtritis Beach

What Happens: The Sultan's royal family sends offerings to the volcano or sea—symbolic gifts to the spirits believed to protect the land.

How to Get There

Mount Merapi: Scooter (Rp 80,000/day) or local tour (\~Rp 150,000)

Parangtritis Beach: GoJek or public bus from Giwangan Terminal (\~Rp 15,000–50,000)

Why It Matters: It's a powerful reminder of how deeply Javanese people respect nature and the spiritual world. It's not performed for show—it's a prayer in motion.

Grebeg Maulud

Where: Starts at the Kraton, winds through town

What Happens: A giant cone of food is paraded through the streets, then torn apart by excited locals—it's believed to bring good fortune.

Cost: Free

Traveler Tip: Go early, bring a hat, and be ready for crowds. It's chaotic in the best way.

Practical information

Religion and tradition in Yogyakarta aren't placed away or commercialized. They're felt in the morning breeze, in the hum of a gamelan, in the stories shared by candlelight. Open your heart, take your time, and let this city show you how the past and present can coexist beautifully.

You're not just witnessing culture—you're being invited into it.

Cultural Etiquette

Do's, Don'ts & Respecting Local Customs

Yogyakarta isn't just a place you see—it's a place you feel. It's rich in tradition, soaked in stories, and filled with people who carry centuries of culture in the way they greet you, share a meal, or open their homes. And when you visit, you're not just a tourist—you're a guest. So, let's talk about a few gentle customs that'll help you fit in, make new friends, and experience Yogyakarta in its most genuine form.

The Do's (Small Gestures, Big Meaning)

- **Smile and bow your head a little when greeting others.**

It's simple, but powerful. A warm smile and a slight nod of respect—especially to elders—go a long way in showing you're not just passing through, but genuinely here.

- **Use your right hand for giving and receiving.**

From handing over money at a market to receiving a delicious plate of gudeg, always try to use your right hand. It's a quiet sign of respect that locals notice and appreciate.

- **Take your shoes off before entering someone's home or certain buildings.**

If you spot shoes lined up outside, yours should join them. It's a small gesture, but one that says, "I see your space—and I respect it."

- **Dress modestly, especially in cultural or religious sites.**

You don't have to be covered from head to toe, but think light, breathable clothing that covers shoulders and knees. You'll be more comfortable, and you'll blend in better.

- **Ask before snapping someone's photo.**

A simple "Boleh foto?" with a kind smile will almost always earn you a yes—and sometimes even a pose. It's a moment of human connection, not just content for Instagram.

The Don'ts (What to Avoid Without Stressing Out)

- **Don't point your feet at people or sacred objects.**

In Java, feet are considered the "lowest" part of the body—not just physically. If you're sitting on the floor, try to place your feet away politely. Don't worry, locals won't scold you—they'll just appreciate the effort.

- **Avoid touching someone's head—even little kids.**

Heads are considered sacred, the highest point of the body. A head pat might seem playful where you're from, but here, it's best avoided unless you know the person well.

- **Keep the romance private.**

Hand-holding is okay, especially in tourist areas, but kissing or hugging in public is still a bit taboo. In rural villages or religious sites, even more so. Think of it as saving a little magic just for the two of you.

- **Avoid raising your voice or being confrontational.**

In Javanese culture, calmness is a virtue. Even when something's frustrating (yes, even that bus delay), take a deep breath. A calm tone gets you more help—and more respect.

- **Respecting Sacred Sites (Temples & Palaces)**

Whether you're wandering the awe-inspiring Borobudur, the graceful towers of Prambanan, or the dignified Kraton (Sultan's Palace), remember: these aren't just photo ops—they're sacred.

Dress the part: Cover your shoulders and knees. Sarongs are often available at the entrance if needed.

Follow the flow: Walk where others walk. Avoid restricted areas, even if they look tempting.

Lower your voice: A soft tone speaks volumes in places of reverence.

How to Get to These Sacred Spaces

Borobudur Temple

Location: Magelang Regency (approx. 40 km from Yogyakarta)

Getting there: Join a sunrise tour (from Rp 150,000+), take a public bus from Jombor Terminal (Rp 25,000–35,000), or rent a scooter (\~Rp 80,000/day).

Best time to go: Early morning for fewer crowds and golden light.

Prambanan Temple

Location: Just 17 km east of downtown Yogyakarta

Getting there: Take Trans Jogja Line 1A (Rp 4,000), GoJek (\~Rp 30,000–40,000), or join a guided tour.

Tip: Sunset views here are absolutely magical.

Kraton (Sultan's Palace)

Location: Right in the heart of the city

Getting there: Walk, cycle, or hop in a traditional back (Rp 20,000–30,000 depending on distance).

Entry: Around Rp 15,000 for foreigners.

Practical information

No one expects you to be flawless. You'll probably slip up—and that's okay. What matters most in Yogyakarta is your intention. If you're kind, curious, and show respect, people will embrace you with open arms. And that's when the real magic happens.

Because in Yogyakarta, it's not just what you see—it's how you make people feel. And when you show a little heart, this beautiful city gives it right back.

PRACTICAL TIPS & ESSENTIAL INFO

SIM Cards, Internet & Staying Connected

Let's be honest—whether you're navigating your way through Yogyakarta's charming alleyways, uploading temple selfies, or just checking in with family back home, staying connected is super important. The good news? It's really easy (and cheap!) to get yourself online here.

Where to Get a SIM Card

The moment you touch down at Adisutjipto International Airport (JOG), you'll see a few stalls in the arrivals area offering tourist SIM cards. They're fast, convenient, and will have you connected before your luggage even hits the carousel. That said, if you're okay waiting a bit, heading to a proper store in the city can save you a little money and give you more options.

Look for official outlets like Telkomsel, XL Axiata, or Indosat Ooredoo. You can find these at malls like Ambarukmo Plaza, Malioboro Mall, or even smaller convenience shops around the city. Just make sure it's an authorized shop—some street vendors may charge extra or skip the required SIM registration process.

Which Provider Should You Choose?

Telkomsel: Best coverage and fastest data—great if you're heading to beaches or rural spots.

XL Axiata: Good value with solid coverage in town.

Indosat Ooredoo: Budget-friendly option with fair performance.

How Much Does It Cost?

A standard SIM card with 5–10 GB of data usually costs between IDR 50,000–100,000 (that's roughly \$3–\$7 USD). Enough to keep your Instagram stories flowing and your maps working!

The seller will usually set everything up for you—including registration and activation. If they don't, just smile and say:

Bisa bantu aktivasi kartu saya?" (Bee-sah bahn-too sah-yah) – Can you help activate my SIM card?

Pocket Wi-Fi

A Group-Friendly Option

Traveling with friends or family? Renting a pocket Wi-Fi might be even easier.

- You can pre-book through sites like Traveloka or Klook.
- The daily cost is around IDR 70,000 (\$4.50 USD).
- Pick it up at the airport or have it delivered to your hotel.

Either way, you'll be all set for that photo of Borobudur at sunrise, or tracking down the nearest warung with rave reviews.

Currency Exchange & Tipping Etiquette

Let's be real — no matter how beautiful a place is, if you're confused about money, it can add stress to your trip. But don't worry — in Yogyakarta, managing your budget is refreshingly simple and won't break the bank (unless you go wild with batik shopping — hey, no judgment!).

What's the Currency Like?

Indonesia uses the Rupiah (IDR), and yes, there are a lot of zeros — but don't let that scare you!

Just remember:

IDR 10,000 is about \$0.65 USD

IDR 100,000 is around \$6.50 USD

You'll be handling lots of colorful bills, from bright red IDR 100,000s to smaller green and blue notes.

Pro tip: Organize your cash early on — it helps you avoid overpaying, especially at busy markets or in taxis where things can move fast.

Exchanging Money

Where and How

If you're bringing foreign cash, don't just hand it to the first person waving a calculator — here's how to exchange wisely:

Banks: Reliable and safe, though not the fastest. Great for large sums. Bring your passport.

Authorized Money Changers: Found easily around Malioboro Street, Prawirotaman, and near touristy areas. Look for official signage — and avoid those "Pssst! Money change?" offers in the alleyways.

ATMs: A traveler's best friend. Widely available and often easiest. Look for ATMs attached to banks or inside malls. Most accept Visa/Mastercard and dispense between IDR 2–3 million (\$130–\$200) per withdrawal.

Pro tip

Always choose "withdraw in local currency" at the ATM — it usually gives you a much better exchange rate than converting in your home currency.

What About Cards?

Yogyakarta is catching up fast with digital payments. Many hotels, restaurants, malls, and even some tour services accept credit/debit cards.

But... street food vendors, small family-owned warungs, and most local markets still love good old-fashioned cash.

If you get a local SIM card, you might also be able to use GoPay, OVO, or DANA — popular e-wallet apps. They're especially handy for booking rides or ordering snacks on delivery apps.

To Tip or Not to Tip?

Indonesians don't expect tips, but they always appreciate kindness. Here's a friendly guide for tipping in Yogyakarta:

Restaurants: If service isn't included (check your bill), leave 5–10%.

Hotel Staff: IDR 10,000–20,000 (about \$0.70–\$1.30) for bellhops or housekeeping.

Drivers or Guides: Around IDR 50,000–100,000 per day (\$3–\$6), depending on how awesome they are.

Small cafes/warungs: No need, but rounding up the bill is always nice.

- At the end of the day, tipping is about showing gratitude — not obligation. Even a small tip or a warm "terima kasih" (thank you) can make someone's day.

Recommended Travel Apps & Booking Sites

Whether you're looking for a ride, a cheap place to stay, or a way to book that sunrise tour of Borobudur without speaking a word of Bahasa, these apps can make your trip a whole lot smoother.

And don't worry — you don't need to be a tech wizard. I'll walk you through how to download and use each one.

Getting Around Like a Local

Grab

Think of it as Southeast Asia's Uber — but with more options (like motorbike taxis or even bubble tea delivery).

Why it's helpful: You can book a ride, order food, or even pay at convenience stores.

How to download it

1. Open your phone's App Store (for iPhone) or Google Play Store (for Android).

2. Search for "Grab".

3. Hit Download or Install.

4. Open it, sign up using your phone number, and you're all set.

How much it costs: A 15-minute GrabBike ride around town costs roughly IDR 10,000–15,000 (about \$0.65–\$1 USD).

Gojek

This app does it all — rides, food, massages, laundry pickup, and even movie tickets.

Why people love it: It's affordable and widely used across Indonesia.

Steps to install: Same process — search for "Gojek" in your app store, install it, register, and go!

Pro tip

Choose "cash" as your payment option if you're not using an Indonesian e-wallet.

Booking Places to Stay

Traveloka

This Indonesian app is a local favorite. You can book flights, hotels, trains, and even theme park tickets in one place.

Why it's great: Works well in English, plus offers local deals and coupons.

How to get it

1. Search for "Traveloka" in your app store.

2. Install it and create an account.

3. Start browsing by city, dates, and budget.

Room prices: Budget stays from IDR 100,000–300,000/night (\~\$7–\$20 USD), mid-range from \$25–\$60 USD.

Booking.com, Agoda, & Airbnb

If you're more familiar with these — you're in luck. They work great in Yogyakarta.

How to use them

1. Download the app of your choice.

2. Sign up (if you haven't already).

3. Search "Yogyakarta", select dates, filter by price and type.

4. Done!

- Staying in areas like Malioboro, Prawirotaman, or Kraton puts you close to culture, cafes, and quirky shops.

Booking Activities & Tours

Klook & GetYourGuide

These apps are awesome for finding day trips, cultural experiences, and skip-the-line tickets to temples.

Why they're useful: English-friendly, and they often include hotel pickup.

How to use

1. Download Klook or GetYourGuide.

2. Open the app, create an account (easy with Google or email).

3. Search for Borobudur, batik workshops, or street food tours.

4. Book, pay, and you'll receive an e-ticket instantly.

Withlocals

Want something more personal? This one connects you with real locals offering everything from market tours to home-cooked meals.

How to get started: Just like the others — download, sign up, browse by category, and message your host.

Breaking the Language Barrier

Google Translate

It's more than just a translator — it can actually scan signs and menus with your phone's camera.

<u>How to download</u>

1. Look for "Google Translate" in your app store.

2. Install it and open the app.

3. Download the Bahasa Indonesia language pack so you can use it offline (helpful when you're out of signal).

Cool trick: Tap the camera icon, hover over a menu or sign, and the words turn into English — like magic.

Health Tips & Vaccination Info

Because nothing ruins a vacation faster than feeling under the weather.

So, you've packed your camera, sunscreen, and sense of adventure — great! But let's make sure you pack a little peace of mind too. Staying healthy in Yogyakarta isn't hard, but it does take a bit of prep. Here's how to feel your best while exploring everything from bustling markets to quiet rice fields.

Before You Fly

The Jab Talk

Let's start with the least exciting part — vaccines. Nobody likes them, but trust me, getting a quick jab now is way better than dealing with a fever in a homestay with no air-con.

Recommended vaccines for Indonesia

- Hepatitis A – because you'll be eating some incredible street food.
- Hepatitis B – just in case. Better safe than sorry.

- Typhoid – same reason as Hep A: food and water safety.
- Tetanus – keep this one updated. Accidents happen.
- Rabies – consider this if you'll be hiking, cycling, or hanging out in villages with lots of dogs or monkeys.
- COVID-19 vaccines are still a good idea — some places or airlines might require proof, and it helps protect everyone.

Try to visit your doctor or a travel clinic about 4–6 weeks before you leave, just to give your body time to adjust.

What to Pack in Your Mini First-Aid Kit

You don't need to bring a pharmacy, but a few basics can really save the day. Here's what seasoned travelers usually stash in their bag:

- Pain relief (like Panadol or Ibuprofen)
- Rehydration salts (a must for hot days or upset tummies)
- Anti-diarrhea meds (Loperamide is your friend)

- Allergy tablets (just in case the local pollen or a bug bite acts up)
- Insect repellent (a strong one — dengue is a thing)
- Hand sanitizer (the mini bottle that goes everywhere with you)
- Band-aids and a small antiseptic cream (for cuts or blisters)

Tip: Always keep your meds in their original packaging — customs officers appreciate that.

Mosquitoes, Dengue & the Buzz About Malaria

Malaria risk in Yogyakarta is very low. So don't stress about taking malaria pills unless you're heading into remote jungles.

But dengue fever? That's a bit more common, especially during rainy season (around November to March). Don't worry — it's preventable.

Here's how to outsmart the mozzies:

- Wear long sleeves and pants at dawn and dusk

- Use a strong mosquito repellent daily (DEET or picaridin-based)
- Sleep under a mosquito net if you're out in the countryside or in rustic places

Safe Food & Water

Yogyakarta has some of the best food in Southeast Asia, hands down. But your stomach might need a day or two to adjust.

Keep it happy by following these tips

- Drink bottled water only (and check the seal)
- Skip the ice unless you know it's from filtered water
- Eat hot, fresh food — if it's sizzling on the grill, go for it
- Avoid raw salads or fruit that's already been cut and left out
- Trust the crowd: If locals are lining up, that's your spot

Your taste buds are going to love this place — just take it one sambal at a time!

Stay Hydrated & Don't Overdo It

Indonesia is hot and humid — you'll sweat more than you think. Be kind to yourself:

- Drink lots of water (yes, again)
- Wear a hat and light clothing
- Slow down during the hottest hours (12–3 PM)
- Don't skip meals — food is fuel
- Listen to your body. If you're tired, rest. You're on vacation!

Hospitals, Clinics & Pharmacies

Let's talk about something we hope you won't need—but should definitely know just in case.

Whether it's an upset stomach from too much spicy sambal, a twisted ankle after hiking, or just a nagging cold, it's comforting to know that Yogyakarta has reliable healthcare facilities. From modern private hospitals to 24-hour pharmacies, you're in good hands here.

Where to Go When You Need Medical Help

1. RSUP Dr. Sardjito (Public Hospital)

Location: Jl. Kesehatan, Sekip, Sleman

Phone number: +62 274 587333

Time: Open 24/7

This is one of the biggest government hospitals in Yogyakarta. It's well-equipped and sees a lot of local patients, so it might be busy, but the care is solid. English may be limited, so having a translation app or a bilingual local nearby can really help.

2. Siloam Hospitals Yogyakarta (Private)

Location: Jl. Laksda Adisucipto No.32-34, Demangan

Contact: +62 274 487 888

Time: Open 24/7

This is a favorite among international travelers. It's clean, modern, and many of the doctors and staff speak English. It's a private hospital, so expect to pay up front unless your travel insurance covers it directly—keep your receipts just in case.

3. Bethesda Hospital

Location: Jl. Jend. Sudirman No.70, Gondokusuman

Phone number: +62 274 586688

Time: Open 24/7

An old and well-respected hospital that many locals trust. It's also a great option if you're staying near the city center.

Picking Up Medications

Need some pain relievers, cold medicine, or just some mosquito repellent? Pharmacies (called "Apotek" in Indonesian) are everywhere.

- Guardian – Easy to spot in malls like Malioboro Mall or Ambarrukmo Plaza.
- Kimia Farma – A well-known chain found across the city.
- Apotek K-24 – Open 24 hours, every day. Perfect for late-night needs.

Tip: If you're unsure what medicine to get, show them a photo or packaging of what you're used to—they'll usually find the equivalent for you.

In Case of an Emergency

If something serious happens, here's what to do:

1. Call 119 for a government ambulance.

2. If you want quicker service (and you're near a private hospital), call the hospital directly—they often send their own ambulance.

3. Have your passport and travel insurance details with you—they'll likely ask for them at check-in.

4. Don't panic. If you're in a hotel or guesthouse, ask the front desk to help—they're usually great in emergencies.

Important Numbers (Save These Somewhere Safe)

Ambulance: 119

Police: 110

Fire Dept: 113

Tourist Info: +62 274 555 585

Emergency Numbers & Contacts

Let's be real—nobody wants to need this page. But if you do, you'll be glad it's here.

Whether it's a sudden health issue, a lost passport, or just a travel hiccup you didn't see coming, it helps to have the right numbers handy. This is your little lifeline section—save it to your phone, write it in your notebook, or screenshot it now.

Key Emergency Numbers in Indonesia

These are the ones you'll want to memorize or have at your fingertips:

Ambulance:　　　119

Police:　　　110

Fire Department:　113

General Emergency (Mobile Users):　112

Note: Dialing 112 from a mobile phone works in most areas, even if you don't have credit or an active SIM card. It's your best bet for urgent help.

Need a Doctor? Here's Where to Go

If you find yourself needing medical attention—don't panic. Yogyakarta has some well-equipped hospitals that cater to locals and travelers alike.

RSUP Dr. Sardjito: (Government hospital, 24/7 service)

Location: Jl. Kesehatan No.1, Sekip

Phone number: +62 274 587333

Siloam Hospitals Yogyakarta: (Private, English-speaking staff available)

Location: Jl. Laksda Adisucipto No.32-34

Phone number: +62 274 487 888

Bethesda Hospital: (Trusted by many locals)

Location: Jl. Jend. Sudirman No.70

Phone number: +62 274 586688

Tip: Hotel receptionists can often help you call a taxi or arrange transport if you're unwell or unsure of how to get there.

Tourist Police

Yes, They're a Real Thing (and Super Helpful)

If your wallet goes missing, you're feeling unsafe, or you just need some travel help, the Tourist Police are there for you.

Tourist Police Malioboro Post

Located near the Tourist Info Center on Jl. Malioboro

Phone number: +62 274 563 681

They speak basic English and are used to helping visitors—so don't hesitate!

Tourist Information Center (TIC)

Location: Jl. Malioboro No.16

Phone number: +62 274 555 585

Time: Open daily: 9 AM – 4 PM

Friendly, helpful staff—great for quick advice, directions, or booking help.

Embassies & Consulates

Lost your passport? Need consular help? Most embassies are based in Jakarta, but they're just a phone call or email away. Below are the big ones:

U.S. Embassy: +62 21 5083 1000

UK Embassy: +62 21 2356 5200

Australian Embassy: +62 21 2550 5555

Canadian Embassy: +62 21 2550 7800

German Embassy: +62 21 3985 5000

Need to find your country's embassy? Head to:

https://www.embassypages.com

Sustainable Travel Tips

Travel isn't just about the places you go—it's about the way you go.

Yogyakarta welcomes you with its centuries-old temples, handmade batik, flavorful street eats, and the genuine smiles of its people. But let's face it: tourism changes things. That's why traveling responsibly isn't just nice—it's necessary. And the good news? It doesn't take a lot to make a difference.

Here are some super doable ways to tread a little lighter and leave a positive mark behind.

1. Be Water-Wise

Water might seem endless when you're showering after a hot day, but it's a limited resource in many parts of Java.

- Keep showers short (even if they feel amazing).
- Turn off the tap while brushing your teeth.
- Reuse your hotel towels instead of asking for fresh ones daily.

Look for hotels or cafés that offer water refill stations—it's cheaper, greener, and just makes sense!

2. Cut Down on Plastic

Plastic is everywhere in Southeast Asia—and it piles up quickly. But you can help cut it down, one bottle or straw at a time.

- Bring a reusable water bottle. Bonus points if it has a filter.
- Carry your own reusable bag and say no to plastic bags.
- Learn this lifesaver: "Tidak pakai sedotan" (tee-dahk pah-KAI suh-DOH-tan) – "No straw, please."

Pro tip: Say it with a smile—locals appreciate the effort.

3. Support the Local Good Stuff

When you buy from street vendors, small shops, or artists, your money goes directly to families—not big corporations.

- Look for handmade crafts instead of factory-made souvenirs.
- Choose homestays or guesthouses over large chain hotels.
- Eat at family-run warungs or local cafés.
- Batik made by hand takes time and skill—ask the vendor about it. You'll hear amazing stories.

4. Go Slow, Go Local

Traffic can be wild in the city center, but you don't always need to be in a car. Sometimes, the best way to see Yogyakarta is by slowing down.

- Walk, rent a bike, or hop on a becak (pedicab).
- Going further? Take the train—it's affordable and scenic.
- Share rides with Grab or Gojek if you need to use a car.

Pedaling through the rice fields near Prambanan at sunset? Unreal.

5. Show Some Respect

Temples and ceremonies are more than photo ops—they're part of daily life here. A little respect goes a long way.

- Cover your shoulders and knees when visiting temples or villages.
- Ask before snapping someone's photo—especially elders or street performers.
- Watch how locals behave and follow their lead.

Golden rule: if it feels invasive, it probably is.

6. Choose Experiences That Give Back

Want to connect with Yogyakarta on a deeper level? Join a cooking class, learn batik from a master, or stay with a local family.

Look for activities that:
- Are locally owned and operated.
- Give part of their earnings back to the community.
- Encourage cultural exchange—not just entertainment.

Imagine learning how to make gudeg in someone's home kitchen... That's a memory you'll keep forever.

7. Learn Before You Go

A little prep can really elevate your experience. Learn a few Bahasa phrases, read up on the culture, and brush up on what's polite (and what's not).

Even a simple "Terima kasih" (thank you) can earn you a big smile.

Small Choices, Big Impact

You don't have to be a perfect eco-warrior to travel responsibly. Just be mindful. Be curious. Be kind. Your trip will feel more meaningful—and your hosts will feel more respected.

Leave footprints, take memories... and maybe a few new friendships too."

CONCLUSION

So here we are—at the end of the guide, but hopefully, just the beginning of your journey. Whether you were flipping through these pages during your planning stages or reading it with a kopi joss in hand from a street-side warung, I hope this book felt more like a friendly companion than a list of travel tips.

Yogyakarta is not the kind of place you just visit and leave behind. It sticks with you—in the little things. The way the morning light spills over the temples. The sound of kids laughing near a food cart. The kind eyes of a local who helps you navigate the bus system when you're clearly confused. It's all these ordinary moments that somehow become extraordinary memories.

My goal wasn't just to show you where to go and what to eat. It was to help you connect—with the place, with the people, and maybe even with a part of yourself you haven't met yet. From spicy gudeg and colorful batik workshops to quiet moments watching a shadow puppet show, Yogyakarta has a way of welcoming you like family—even if you arrived as a stranger.

And if you've made it this far, thank you.

Really, writing this guide wasn't just about maps and recommendations—it was about sharing a place I've come to admire, and helping you fall in love with it too.

So here's what I'll leave you with: Don't over-plan. Leave space for the surprises. Smile at strangers. Ask questions. Try things that scare you a little. And above all—enjoy it all. The missteps. The perfect moments. The unexpected magic.

Because that's what Yogyakarta does best. It welcomes you in, changes your perspective, and sends you home with stories you'll be telling for years.

Until then—safe travels, new friends.

And who knows? Maybe one day, your journey will bring you back here again.

Printed in Dunstable, United Kingdom